D1735350

Air Force Badges and Insignia
of World War 2

Guido Rosignoli

Air Force Badges and Insignia of World War 2

Great Britain, Norway, Netherlands, U.S.S.R.,
Denmark, France, Belgium, Yugoslavia,
U.S.A., Italy, China, Bulgaria,
Germany, Czechoslovakia, Finland, Poland,
Japan, Rumania, Hungary

BLANDFORD PRESS
Poole   Dorset

Set in Monotype Plantin 9/10pt
*Printed and bound in Great Britain by
Cox & Wyman Ltd, London,
Fakenham and Reading*

Contents

Introduction

In the first decade of this century, on Sundays—weather permitting—a man used to fly in a 'peculiar machine' over the fields surrounding a small town in the Kustenland province of the Austro–Hungarian Empire.

'That was Mr Russian, a local man,' my Aunt in later years told me. 'We used to go to watch him flying and we just couldn't believe our eyes. Some people thought he was mad, but I don't know! He was more like a genius.'

Then in World War 2, many aeroplanes approached the town; they were shiny, tiny objects, high up in the sky; one could not believe there were men inside controlling them. There was a great whistling noise and her house, with all her belongings, disappeared in seconds. The world had travelled a long way since the first flights of Mr Russian's 'peculiar machine'.

The pioneers of flight could hardly have foreseen the development of their machines, nor their eventual deadly use. Civilian aviation developed too, but only as a consequence of progress in the military field. The aircraft was deployed in and has conquered its own environment, the sky, whereas the motor car has made less comparative progress since motorways have never been designed to anticipate its full development.

If aircraft are the 'tools' of aviation, badges are its heraldry. But as the history of aviation is short, it would be incorrect and misleading in this book to deal only with the badges worn during World War 2, as in most cases these were a development of others worn previously. Some badges were adopted in the 1920s, or even earlier. Therefore, historical background information has been added where possible.

Some nations have developed their air forces as a separate service, others as a complement to the existing services. In the latter case it has often been difficult to separate aviation badges from those of the parent service as, obviously, badges that technically belonged to the Army and the Navy were also worn by aviators. Often it has been difficult to reach a compromise but I hope that readers will find this book a balanced approach to its subject and become interested in a relatively neglected field.

Guido Rosignoli,
Farnham, Surrey,
1976

To
K. Barbarski

Acknowledgments

I would like to thank:
Mr H. L. King; Mr A. L. Kipling; Mr S. L. Nash; Mr E. E. Stott, Royal Aircraft Establishment, Farnborough; Prof. C. Thomas, M.A., F.S.A., Hon. M.R.I.A., and Mr A. E. White.

Squadron Leader A. J. Cockle, H.Q. Rhodesian Air Force, Salisbury; Major L. N. Masencamp of the Office of the Armed Forces Attaché at the South African Embassy, London, and Major C. A. Morrison, Canadian Defence Liaison Staff in London.

Mr A. Kielland Hauge, Curator of the Haermuseet, Oslo.

Captain H. Ringoir, Hon. Gunner of the R.N.A.

Mr L. A. T. Ege, Director of the Royal Danish Air Force's Historical Branch and Mrs Inga Fl. Rasmussen, Curator, Tøjhusmuseet, Copenhagen; and Mr J. P. Champagne.

P. M. Pavasovic, Lieut.-Col. Royal Yugoslav Artillery, President of the Royal Yugoslav ex-Combatants' Association 'Drazha Mihailovich' in Great Britain, and his son Mr Milan P. Pavasovic, who was responsible for translations and the organisation of the material relating to the Royal Yugoslav Air Force.

Mr C. G. Sweeting, Curatorial Assistant, Aeronautics, at the National Air and Space Museum, Smithsonian Institution, Washington D.C. and Mr Pierre C. T. Vereye.

Col. Pilota G. Battazzi, Air Force Attaché at the Italian Embassy in London, and Geom. L. Granata.

Lieut.-General, CA, Chang Ju-ho, Deputy Chief of General Staff for Personnel, Ministry of National Defence, Republic of China.

Mr A. Mollo; Mr F. Ollenschläger and G. I. Paprikoff, M.D.

Mr M. Melkko, Director, Sotamuseo, Helsinki; Commander I. Balaban, Mr I. Ratiu, M.A., LL.B.

Mr K. Barbarski, Vice Curator of the Polish Institute and Sikorski Museum in London; Captain W. Milewski and Lieut.-Colonel B. Mincer. Lastly my thanks to Diana, my wife, for her assistance.

Great Britain

Plate 1. Historical Background

The first aeronautic venture of significance began in the late 1870s with the setting up of a Balloon School at Chatham and soon after interest was captured by airships, the next obvious stage of flight.

Meanwhile a great deal of individual efforts were dedicated to the building of aeroplanes, until finally, in April 1911, the Air Battalion, Royal Engineers, was officially formed at Farnborough. It was divided in two detachments, one specialised in airships, the other in aeroplanes. Other experiments had taken place at Eastchurch where the Naval Flying School was established in 1911.

In order to unify these disjointed efforts a Royal Warrant was issued on 13 April 1912 sanctioning the formation of the Royal Flying Corps, with a Naval and a Military Wing, both served by the same Flying School. However, the Royal Navy kept its own school at Eastchurch and eventually on 1 July 1914 the Naval Wing of the Royal Flying Corps became the Royal Naval Air Service.

At the outbreak of World War 1 there were no armed aircraft in Britain and the first experiments with machine-guns took place in the following year, 1915. Initially, the only flyers were pilots and observers but during the war the observer also became air gunner.

Pilots wings, in gilt metal with brooch pin at the back, and in embroidery, were granted in 1913 for full dress and service dress, respectively. The observers obtained their own badge (Plate 3) in September 1915.

The cap and collar badges of the Royal Flying Corps resemble those of the Royal Engineers, the forerunners of British aviation, while the cap badges of the Royal Naval Air Service maintained their naval flair, with an eagle in flight in place of the anchor. The personnel of the latter wore naval uniforms; the flying officers wore the eagle on the left sleeve above the distinction lace and, from 1916, also on the left shoulder board. The observers were given their own badge in 1917, a winged 'O' which was worn on both sleeves and shoulder straps. Later in the same year a winged 'A' was adopted for officers of the Royal Naval Reserve and Royal Naval Volunteer Reserve attached to the Royal Naval Air Service.

Many other badges were introduced during World War 1: ratings wore a red embroidered eagle on the right sleeve and specialists had propellers and other devices placed under their eagles. Metal and cloth shoulder titles and other badges were also adopted, even cap tallies inscribed 'ROYAL FLYING CORPS' in gold standard lettering on black.

The Royal Flying Corps, Military Wing, had its own uniforms from 1913, with an unusual double breasted service dress tunic which was known as the 'maternity jacket'. During World War I the officers wore their rank badges on the shoulder straps or alternatively on the cuffs.

There were two classes of warrant officer, wearing the Royal Arms and the Royal Crown respectively. The Quartermaster-Sergeant had four inverted chevrons ensigned by the propeller of the Flight Sergeant who had three 'V' chevrons, with a 4-bladed prop- and star-badge as illustrated, and the Royal Crown above. Only the propeller, without its central star, was worn by the Sergeant and two chevrons, without any badge, were worn by the Corporal. In October 1916, a new badge was adopted for Air Mechanic First Class: it depicted a 2-bladed propeller, embroidered in white on khaki, worn on the right upper sleeve above the elbow.

The officers wore metal R.F.C. shoulder titles while other ranks wore cloth titles, embroidered in white on dark blue.

The growth of aviation during World War I is remarkable. In August 1914 the personnel of the R.F.C. amounted to 1,244 officers and other ranks while the personnel of the R.N.A.S. comprised a total of about 600 men, flying 272 machines in all. By October 1918 the R.A.F. comprised over 290,000 officers and other ranks manning 198 squadrons and five flights.

At the beginning of that war no one yet knew if the future of aviation lay in the aeroplane or in the airship. Aeroplanes were all-purpose machines, classified by their speed and reliability and by the end of the war there were fighter-interceptors, bombers, observation planes and even aeroplanes for long-range reconnaissance.

New, skilled men were required for this type of warfare: Marconi's 'apparatus' was fitted on the planes so that messages could be transmitted and received and the wireless operators began wearing a brass badge depicting an 'O' for operator, with three lightning flashes on each side. Photographers were trained for aerial observation.

It was the age of the great aces of aviation, who surged to fame by destroying scores of enemy planes; for example, Captain Albert Ball V.C. and Major W. Avery Bishop, V.C., a Canadian who shot down at least fifty enemy planes, out-rivalled by Captain James B. McCudden, who by April 1918 had destroyed fifty-four planes. Twice he destroyed four 4-seater enemy planes in a single day.

In the meantime, it became apparent that a general reorganisation was necessary in order to develop, govern and supply adequately this ever growing new war-machine. The Air Board was expanded to Air Ministry and on 1 April 1918 the R.F.C. and the R.N.A.S. combined to form the

Royal Air Force. In 1924 the Fleet Air Arm was instituted and officers of the Royal Navy were admitted to R.A.F. training schools.

Khaki service dress uniforms, similar to those of the army, were adopted in April 1918 and sky blue uniforms made their appearance as well for a short time after the end of the war, until in September 1919 the familiar grey-blue uniforms were finally introduced. New officers' ranks badges were also introduced in 1918: these were cuff stripes of varying size with a crowned eagle above them. The crown and the eagle were in separate pieces and the latter always faced outwards.

The rank titles were then still the same as those of the Army; the generals wore a large stripe with three, two or one narrow stripes above it. The Brigadier-General had only the large stripe while the Colonel and the Lieutenant-Colonel wore four and three narrow stripes respectively. The Major wore two narrow stripes with a narrower one in between (illustrated); the Captain and Lieutenant had two and one stripe respectively and the 2nd Lieutenant initially wore only the crowned eagle on the cuffs and later one narrower stripe as well.

On 27 August 1919 these titles were changed and the colour of the stripes also changed to match the new grey-blue uniforms. These stripes and rank titles are still in use at the present time.

The officers' grey-blue service dress consisted of the peaked cap, a single breasted jacket with open collar, cloth belt and patch pockets with flaps, breeches with puttees or riding boots, or trousers. The other ranks wore tunics with high neck collar until the late 1930s, although warrant officers and senior N.C.O.s had open collars earlier. A couple of years later, breeches and puttees were replaced by trousers for all ranks.

In 1920 a blue full dress uniform was introduced for the officers, followed the year after by a busby of black leather and short fur, in line with the tradition of the original flying helmets. The tunic of this uniform had a stand-up collar with oak leaves embroidered in gold, depending upon rank: officers of Air Rank had embroidery all round the collar; group captains, wing commanders and squadron leaders only at the front, while all others had only five gold oak leaves at the front. All had the crown and eagle in gold on the shoulder straps and the officers of Air rank had an additional laurel wreath around the buttons (Plate 4). A dress waist belt was worn as well.

The greatcoat and mess dress were adopted in 1920, but the latter was abolished during the war, until 1947 when both greatcoat and mess dress were modified. Grey-blue battledress was adopted and worn by all ranks during World War 2.

In 1921 new badges were issued to airmen serving with the Works and Buildings Services, later discontinued in 1929. Among the many old badges of the Commonwealth air forces I have chosen to illustrate the

1920s' pattern of South African pilots' wings, with the Union's coat of arms in its centre.

Canada, Australia, New Zealand and South Africa had their own independent air forces, although many individuals volunteered to join the R.A.F. as did many others who came from British territories where an organised air force did not yet exist.

The Royal Canadian Air Force traces its origins to the Canadian Aviation Corps founded in 1914, which was reorganised in 1920 and became finally an independent service in 1939. A Canadian naval air branch existed for a short time at the end of World War 1 and was re-formed only in 1946.

The Australian Flying Corps was raised in 1913 and although its personnel manned five squadrons during World War 1, the corps was disbanded in 1919. However it was re-formed the following year and in March 1921 it was renamed Australian Air Force, which became 'Royal' a few months later. The Australians wore dark blue uniforms and the officers had gold stripes on the cuffs, below the crowned eagle.

Earlier, during the war, many New Zealanders served in the A.F.C. or in the R.F.C. as the New Zealand Permanent Air Force was raised as late as 1923. It became Royal New Zealand Air Force in 1934 and an independent service three years later.

The South African Aviation Corps was formed in 1915, disbanded in 1918 and re-formed in 1920 under the designation of South African Air Force.

In Rhodesia an Air Unit was formed in 1935, on a Territorial Force basis, as part of the Rhodesia Regiment and after a period of development in May 1938 the first six Rhodesian pilots received their wings. By the end of August 1939, eight aircraft left Salisbury for Nairobi. During the following months, before Italy's entry into the war, many other pilots were trained in Rhodesia and subsequently by the R.A.F. establishment in Iraq.

In April 1940, the Rhodesia Air Force was absorbed into the R.A.F. and No. 1 Squadron became No. 237 (Rhodesia) Squadron. It was deployed in the war against the Italians in Abyssinia, later in North Africa and the Middle East as an army air support unit, which later became a fighter reconnaissance squadron. In the spring of 1944 the squadron was moved to Corsica and operated in Southern France and Northern Italy until its disbandment in 1945.

Rhodesians fought also in the No. 266 Squadron, a unit raised at Sutton Bridge, England, in 1939. It was designated 'Rhodesian' during the Battle of Britain, later taking part in the invasion of Europe and was disbanded at Hildesheim, Germany in August 1945.

Other Rhodesians were employed in Bomber Command units and in

1941 they were grouped into No. 44 Squadron which became therefore another 'Rhodesian' unit of the R.A.F. No. 44 (Rhodesia) Squadron took part in many bombing raids over Germany, among which the daylight raid of 17 April 1942 should be remembered as, of six Rhodesian Lancasters participating in the operation, only one eventually returned.

Great losses were suffered by Rhodesians during World War 2: out of a total of 2,409 aviators 498 were killed and 228 men received decorations and awards. All wore R.A.F. uniforms and insignia with 'RHODESIA' titles on the upper sleeves.

Men of many nationalities, volunteers from the Commonwealth and British territories and exiles from occupied Europe served in the R.A.F. during the war. The latter used R.A.F. grey-blue uniforms, often with their own badges. These have been dealt with in various chapters of this book.

Women served alongside the men in the air force from the beginning of World War 1. The original Women's Royal Air Force was disbanded in 1920 and later, in 1938 women were once again recruited into the Auxiliary Territorial Service, units of which were attached to the R.A.F.; detachments that became eventually the Women's Auxiliary Air Force, with grey-blue uniforms and badges as men, although their rank titles were different. The W.A.A.F. officers and N.C.O.s wore special peaked caps while the other ranks had dark blue berets, later changed to a head-dress similar to that of the former; cap badges were the same as those of the men. Pay was two-thirds that of the men, depending on the duties performed and the rank held. Teleprinter operators, telephonists, mess staff, cooks and M.T. drivers received 1s. 4d. a day on joining, with prospects of 2s. 4d. a day when mustered as aircraftwomen 1st class and higher rates of pay with further promotions. Those entered for certain special duties, such as equipment assistants and clerks, received 2s. 2d. a day on entering, 2s. 8d. a day when mustered as aircraftwomen 1st Class.*

Plate 2. Cap Badges

The official badge of the Royal Air Force, complete with motto was and is still worn by the officers on the busby of the full dress, adopted in 1921. A gold feather-holder is fitted behind this badge attached at the front of the head-dress, made of leather and fur, the latter resembling the ear flaps of the early flying helmets.

The badge originally devised in 1918 included a garter which in 1922 was modified to a circlet; however, the official description of this badge was promulgated by the Air Ministry only in 1949.

When the R.A.F. was formed in 1918, two new designs of cap badges were adopted for officers and other ranks respectively. The generals,

From Hutchinson's *Pictorial History of the War*, Volume 1.

officers and the Warrant Officers 1st Class wore a badge similar to that illustrated for warrant officers on the peaked cap: it was made of brass and mounted upon a padded backing of black cloth. The other ranks wore cap badges similar to those previously worn by those of the R.N.A.S., in gold embroidery for Warrant Officer 2nd Class and N.C.O.s, in worsted embroidery for the others.

Soon after, new cap badges were adopted following the introduction of the new grey-blue service dress uniforms. The officers of Air Rank were distinguished from the other officers by the use of different cap badges and oak leaves on the visor emphasised rank distinction still further.

The regulations of 1918 prescribed the use of upright metal bars at each side of the badge on the cap band. Lieutenants wore one bar while captains wore two bars; field officers had one row of gold oak leaves on the visor and generals were distinguished by two rows of oak leaves. Later, although the two rows of leaves were maintained for the latter, now known as officers of Air Rank, the one row of oak leaves applied to the rank of Group Captain only. All the other officers had a plain visor, lined with grey-blue cloth.

The chaplains had their own badge, a winged Cross Patee in metal below the Royal Crown. The badge, like those of the other officers, was on a padded dark blue backing.

The warrant officers had the same badge as the officers but made of brass and airmen were given a cap badge that closely resembled that of the R.F.C., with different initials in the centre.

The same type of badges and oak leaves embroideries were worn during the last war by the officers and warrant officers of the Commonwealth air forces whose nationality was usually identified by shoulder titles. However, in the case of airmen, the nationality was disclosed by the cap badge as well, usually by means of initials in the centre of the badge. The South Africans had a different pattern of badge altogether, with the eagle in its centre and the initials of the bi-lingual motto on a separate scroll.

The officers wore the eagle below the crown on the left side of the forage cap; this badge was made in one or two pieces and in the latter case the eagle and the crown were attached by means of a brass backing plate in order to keep the same distance between the two. The generals have worn a small replica of the peaked cap's badge since the beginning of World War 2.

The officers wore the eagle below the crown on the left side of the forage cap; this badge was made in one or two pieces and in the latter case the eagle and the crown were attached by means of a brass backing plate in order to keep the same distance between the two. The generals have worn a small replica of the peaked cap's badge since the beginning of World War 2.

HISTORICAL BACKGROUND

Royal Flying Corps
Cap and Collar Badges

Royal Naval Air Service
Officers' Cap Badge

Shoulder Title

Royal Naval Air Service
Chief Petty Officers' Cap Badge

Flight Lieutenant
R.N.A.S.

Flight Observer
R.N.A.S.

Pilot
R.F.C.

Flight Sergeant
R.F.C.

Pilot
South Africa

Shoulder Title

Works and Buildings Services
Cap and Collar Badges

Wireless Operator

Anti-Aircraft Corps
R.N.A.S.

Major R.A.F.
1918–19

Engineer
R.N.A.S.

PLATE 1

GREAT BRITAIN

CAP BADGES

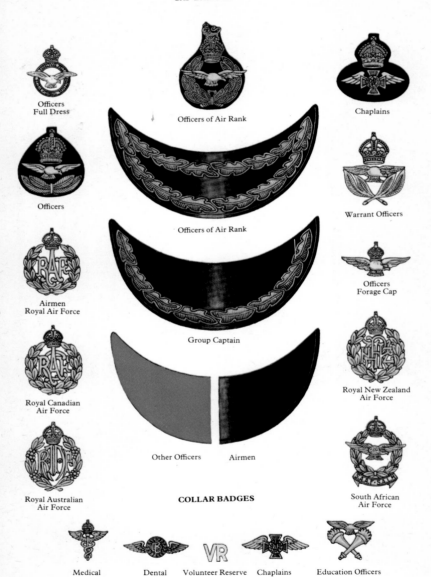

Officers
Full Dress

Officers of Air Rank

Chaplains

Officers

Officers of Air Rank

Warrant Officers

Airmen
Royal Air Force

Group Captain

Officers
Forage Cap

Royal Canadian
Air Force

Royal New Zealand
Air Force

Royal Australian
Air Force

Other Officers   Airmen

South African
Air Force

COLLAR BADGES

Medical   Dental   Volunteer Reserve   Chaplains   Education Officers

PLATE 2

PILOTS' WINGS

Pilot R.A.F.
Service Dress

Pilot R.A.F.
Full Dress

Pilot R.C.A.F.

Pilot R.A.A.F.

Pilot S.A.A.F.

Pilot R.N.Z.A.F.

AIRCREW BADGES – R.A.F.

Observer

Navigator

Air Gunner

Wireless Operator
Air Gunner

Flight Engineer

Bomb Aimer

Parachute Training
Instructor

Signaller

Bomb Aimer

AIRCREW BADGES – R.C.A.F.

Navigator

Bomb Aimer

Air Gunner

Wireless Operator
Air Gunner

Flight Engineer

AIRCREW BADGES – R.A.A.F.

Observer

Air Gunner

Bomb Aimer

Signaller

PLATE 3

GREAT BRITAIN

OFFICERS' RANK BADGES

Officers of Air Rank
Full Dress

Marshal of the Royal Air Force

Other Officers
Full Dress

Air Chief Marshal

Air Marshal

Air Vice-Marshal

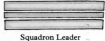

Squadron Leader
Full Dress

Air Commodore

Air Commodore
Full Dress

Group Captain

Wing Commander

Squadron Leader

Flight Lieutenant

Flying Officer

Pilot Officer

Air Marshal
Greatcoat

Flying Officer
Royal Auxiliary Air Force
Battledress

PLATE 4

WARRANT OFFICERS' AND N.C.O.s' RANK BADGES

Warrant Officer
(1st Class)

Flight Sergeant

Sergeant

Corporal

Drum-Major

Leading Aircraftman

Good Conduct Stripes

P.T. Instructor

TRADE AND OTHER BADGES

P.T. Instructor

Bandsman

Shoulder Badge

Trumpeter

Auxiliary

Parachute Training
Instructor

Ground Gunner

Volunteer Reserve

Ground Gunner

Signaller

PLATE 5

GREAT BRITAIN

TRADE AND OTHER BADGES

Combined Operations

R.A.F. Regiment

Air-Sea Rescue Service

Apprentice

Eagle Squadron

Radio Operator/Mechanic

Wireless Operator

Bomb Disposal

Air Gunner

NATIONALITY TITLES

PLATE 6

BADGES OF OTHER FLYING ORGANISATIONS

Air Defence Cadet Corps

Air Transport Auxiliary

Civil Air Guard

Air Transport Auxiliary
Flying Wing

Air Training Corps

Royal Observer Corps

FLEET AIR ARM INSIGNIA

Chief Petty Officers'
Cap Badge

Officers'
Cap Badge

Petty Officers'
Cap Badge

Aircrewman

Observer

Pilot

Telegraphist/Air Gunner
1930–39

Aircrewman (U)

R.A.F. Officers
Attached to F.A.A.

Air Branch Lieutenant
1939

Air Branch Officers
1938

PLATE 7

NON-SUBSTANTIVE BADGES

Rating Observer
1939–45

Acting Rating Observer
1939–45

Air Gunner
1st Class
1939–44

Air Gunner
2nd Class
1939–44

Air Gunner
3rd Class
1939–44

Air Mechanic
Airframes   Engines
1939–48

Radio Mechanic
1944–48

Air Mechanic
Electrical   Ordnance
1939–48

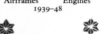

Air Mechanic
Airframes   Engines
1939–48

Radio Mechanic
1944–48

Air Mechanic
Electrical   Ordnance
1939–48

Air Mechanic
Airframes   Engines
1939–48

Qualified Radio Mechanic
1944–47

Air Mechanic
Electrical   Ordnance
1939–48

Air Fitter
Airframes   Engines
1940–48

Air Mechanic
Unclassified
1943–48

Air Fitter
Electrical   Ordnance
1940–48

Airframes   Engines

Air Fitter
Electrical
1940–48

Ordnance

Unclassified
1943–48

PLATE 8

CAP BADGES

General

Officer

Sergeant

Other Ranks

RANK BADGES

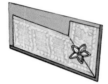

Major-General

Colonel

Lieutenant-Colonel

Major

Captain

Lieutenant

2nd Lieutenant

OTHER BADGES

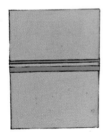

Sergeant

Pilot

Observer

Corporal

Button

PLATE 9

NORWAY

BADGES WORN AFTER 1940

Officers' Nationality Title

Officers' Cap Badge

Airmen Nationality Title

Pilot

Observer

Wireless Operator/Air Gunner

Nationality Badge

Flight Sergeant

Sergeant

Corporal

Leading Aircraftman

NETHERLANDS

ARMY AIR SERVICE – CAP BADGES

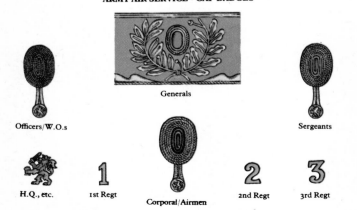

Officers/W.O.s

Generals

Sergeants

H.Q., etc.

1st Regt

Corporal/Airmen

2nd Regt

3rd Regt

PLATE 10

ARMY AIR SERVICE – RANK BADGES

Lieutenant-General   Major-General

Colonel   Lieutenant-Colonel   Major

Captain   1st Lieutenant   2nd Lieutenant

Captain Adjutant   1st Lieutenant Adjutant   Warrant Officer (W.O.1)   Other Ranks

Quartermaster
(upper arm)

Sergeant-Major   Sergeant 1st Class   Sergeant   Corporal

PLATE 11

NETHERLANDS

QUALIFICATION BADGES
ARMY AIR SERVICE

Pilot

Pilot – Observer

Observer

Pilot
(made in Britain)

ROYAL NETHERLANDS INDIAN ARMY
AIR SERVICE

Observer
(made in Britain)

Pilot

Pilot – Observer

Observer

Air Gunner

Flight Surgeon

Bomb Aimer

Photographer

Flight Engineer

Wireless Operator

ROYAL NETHERLANDS NAVAL AIR SERVICE

Air Gunner

Air Telegraphist – Gunner

Telegraphist

TRADE AND OTHER BADGES

R.N.A.A.S.
(nationality title)

Mechanic

Chief Mechanic

Aircraft
Mechanic

Airman attached to R.A.F.V.R.

R.N.A.A.S.
(nationality title)

PLATE 12

RANK BADGES – ARMY AIR SERVICE AFTER 1940

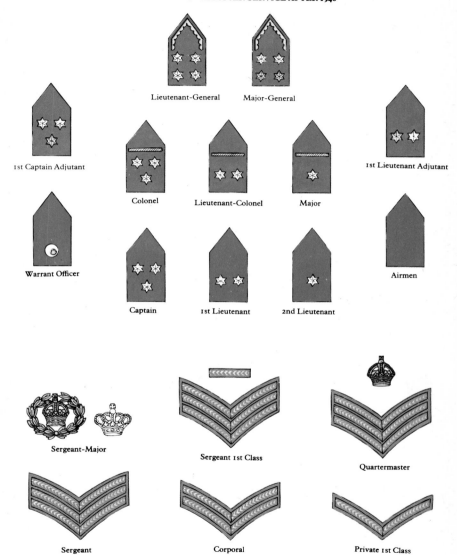

Lieutenant-General   Major-General

1st Captain Adjutant

Colonel   Lieutenant-Colonel   Major

1st Lieutenant Adjutant

Warrant Officer

Captain   1st Lieutenant   2nd Lieutenant

Airmen

Sergeant-Major

Sergeant 1st Class

Quartermaster

Sergeant   Corporal   Private 1st Class

PLATE 13

NETHERLANDS

ROYAL NETHERLANDS NAVAL AIR SERVICE

Flyer
Warrant and Petty Officers

Officers' Cap Badge

Repairman
Warrant and Petty Officers

Repairman
Leading Seaman and
Seaman 1st Class

Repairman
Apprentice 3rd year

Flyer
Corporal
Leading Seaman

Repairman
Apprentice 2nd year

Repairman
Apprentice 1st year

ROYAL NETHERLANDS INDIAN ARMY AIR SERVICE

Captain
Black Uniform

Officers' Cap Badge

Major-General

Major

Garrison Uniform

Colonel
White Uniform

Lieutenant-Colonel
Field Uniform

1st Lieutenant
Garrison Uniform

Ensign
Garrison Uniform

Warrant Officer
Field Uniform

Sergeant-Major
White Uniform

1st Sergeant
Field Uniform

QM Sergeant
Field Uniform

Corporal
Garrison Uniform

PLATE 14

ROYAL NETHERLANDS INDIAN ARMY AIR SERVICE – AFTER 1942

Major-General
collar badge

Officers' Cap Badge

Major-General
shoulder straps' badge

Colonel

Lieutenant-Colonel

Major

Captain

1st Lieutenant

2nd Lieutenant

Ensign

Warrant Officer

Sergeant-Major

Sergeant

Corporal

Private 1st Class

HISTORICAL BACKGROUND U.S.S.R.

Aviation and Aeronautics

Aviation and Aeronautics – Exemplary Unit

Pilot
(Imperial Russian)

Observer
(Imperial Russian)

Red Army Aviator

Red Navy Aviator

Aviation Engineer

PLATE 15

HEAD-DRESS AND RANK BADGES (1940–43)

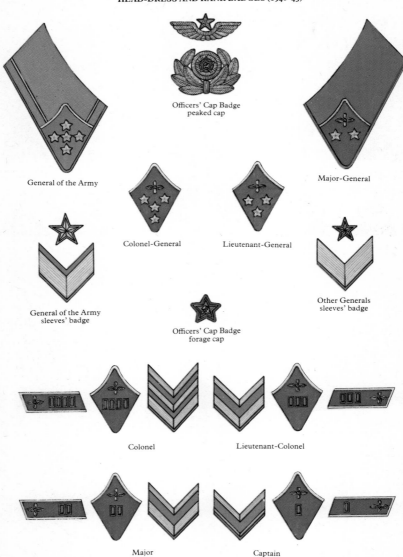

Officers' Cap Badge
peaked cap

General of the Army

Major-General

Colonel-General

Lieutenant-General

General of the Army
sleeves' badge

Other Generals
sleeves' badge

Officers' Cap Badge
forage cap

Colonel

Lieutenant-Colonel

Major

Captain

PLATE 16

RANK BADGES (1940–43)

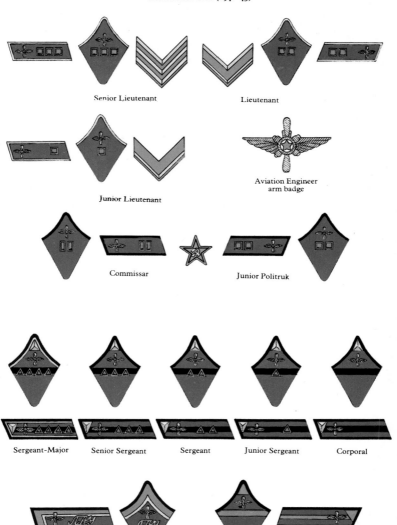

Senior Lieutenant

Lieutenant

Junior Lieutenant

Aviation Engineer
arm badge

Commissar

Junior Politruk

Sergeant-Major Senior Sergeant Sergeant Junior Sergeant Corporal

Aviation School of Leningrad

Military Aviation Service School

PLATE 17

HEAD-DRESS AND RANK BADGES (1943)

Marshals' and Generals' Cap Insignia
(Parade Uniform)

Collar and Cuffs

Collar and Cuffs

Greatcoat Collar Patches
(Parade)   (Ordinary)

Marshals

Generals

Marshals' and Generals' Shoulder Boards

Marshal
4.2.1943

Supreme Marshal
27.10.1943

Marshal
27.10.1943

General of Army

Colonel-General

Lieutenant-General

Major-General

PLATE 18

HEAD-DRESS AND RANK BADGES (1943)

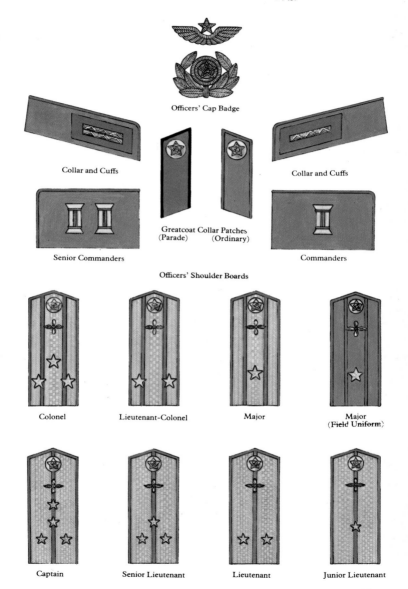

Officers' Cap Badge

Collar and Cuffs

Collar and Cuffs

Greatcoat Collar Patches
(Parade)   (Ordinary)

Senior Commanders

Commanders

Officers' Shoulder Boards

Colonel

Lieutenant-Colonel

Major

Major
(Field Uniform)

Captain

Senior Lieutenant

Lieutenant

Junior Lieutenant

PLATE 19

U.S.S.R.

HEAD-DRESS AND RANK BADGES (1943)

N.C.O.s' Collar

Forage Cap Badge

Privates' Collar

N.C.O.s' Shoulder Boards

| Sergeant-Major | Senior Sergeant | Sergeant | Junior Sergeant | Corporal | Private |

(Parade Uniform)

Sergeant-Major   Corporal

(Field Uniform)

Aviation Specialists' School

DENMARK

MISCELLANEA

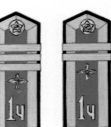

Pilot

Officers attached to R.A.F.V.R.

Airmen Attached to R.A.F.V.R.

PLATE 20

ARMY OF THE AIR – CAP BADGES

General Member
of the Superior War Council
or Air Army Commander

General Commander
of Region or Air Corps

General of Air Division

General of Air Brigade

Metropolitan

North African

General Staff – Captain

Colonial Aviation – Captain

Rank and File

Mechanic/Specialist Officers

Steel Helmet's Badge

Administrative Officers

QUALIFICATION WINGS

Aviation – General Staff

Aviation Metropolitan and North African

Aerodrome – Metropolitan

Aerodrome – North African

(Evening Dress)

Aviation – Colonial

PLATE 21

FRANCE

RANK BADGES

General Member
of the Superior War Council
or Air Army Commander

General Commander
of Region or Air Corps

General of Air Division

General of Air Brigade

Colonel

Lieutenant-Colonel

Major

Captain

Lieutenant

2nd Lieutenant

Chief Warrant Officer

Warrant Officer

Chief-Sergeant

Sergeant
(Regular)

Sergeant

Chief-Corporal

Corporal

Private 1st Class

Chief-Sergeant
(Field Uniform)

PLATE 22

COLLAR PATCHES – OFFICERS

Mechanic/Specialists

Administration

NON-COMMISSIONED OFFICERS

Fighter Interceptors
Pilot

Mixed Formations
Air Crew

North African A.C.
Ground Specialist

Meteorology

RANK AND FILE

Fighter Interceptors

Mixed Formations

Bombers

Intelligence, Reconnaissance,
Observation

Aerodrome
Base (Aircraft)

Aerostation
Base (Balloons)

Balloon
Battalions

Air Battalions
and Companies

North African
Formations

Colonial
Aviation

Meteorology

Mechanic
Aptitude Certificate

Aerostation Stevedore

PLATE 23

FRANCE

QUALIFICATION BADGES – ARMY OF THE AIR

Observer
Cadet Aircraft Pilot

Aircraft Pilot

Air Crew

Airship Pilot

Observer – Mechanic
Cadet Airship Pilot

MARITIME AVIATION

Aircraft Pilot

Arm Badge

Airship Pilot

Aircraft Crew

Captive Balloon
Observer

Pilot Naval Aviation
F.F.N.F.

Aircrew Naval Aviation
F.F.N.F.

FREE FRENCH AIR FORCE

F.F.A.F. Badge

Officers' Cap Badge

F.F.A.F. Badge

Ile-de-France
Group ·

Alsace
Group

Helmet Badge

Lorraine
Group

Bretagne
Group

PLATE 24

FREE FRENCH AIR FORCE

Shoulder Title
Group Normandy in the U.S.S.R.

Military Airline

Shoulder Title
Group Normandy in the U.S.S.R.

Flying Cadre

Shoulder Title
Group Normandy in the U.S.S.R.

Air Mechanics Corps

Air Medical Service

Air Police

Corps of the Administrative Services

Flight Surgeon

Air Commissar

Air Police

Air Musician

Mechanic

Equipment Mechanic

Aircraft Mechanic

Sergeant-Major

N.C.O.s' RANK BADGES

Chief-Sergeant

Sergeant
(Regular)

Sergeant

Chief-Corporal

Corporal

Private 1st Class

PLATE 25

BELGIUM

OFFICERS' CAP AND QUALIFICATION BADGES

Cap Badges

Pilots' Badge 1916–34

1916

1934

Pilots' Badge 1934–48

OFFICERS' RANK BADGES

Ground Personnel

Lieutenant-General

Major-General

Pilots' School

Colonel

Lieutenant-Colonel

Major

Captain Commandant

Captain

Lieutenant

2nd Lieutenant
Ground Personnel

Warrant Officer
1st Class

Warrant Officer

N.C.O.s' RANKS AND OTHER BADGES

Sergeant-Major

1st Sergeant

Sergeant

Corporal

Private 1st Class

Officers attached to
R.A.F.V.R.

Aerostat Officer

Airmen attached to
R.A.F.V.R.

PLATE 26

FORMATIONS' BADGES

Pilots' School

1/I/1
La Mouette

3/II/1
Feuille de Houx

5/III/1
Hirondelle

Aviation School

7/IV/1
Diable

9/V/1
Sioux Bleu

11/VI/1
Sioux Rouge

1/I/2
Comète

2/I/2
Chardon

4/II/2
Cocotte Rouge

3/II/2
Cocotte Blanche

5/III/2
Aigle Bleu

6/III/2
Aigle Rouge

1/I/3
Dragon Doré

3/I/3
Dragon Argenté

5/III/2
Aigle Egyptien

7/III/3
Flèche Ailée

CAP AND QUALIFICATION BADGES

YUGOSLAVIA

Pilot

Officers' Cap Badge

Observer

PLATE 27

YUGOSLAVIA

RANK BADGES

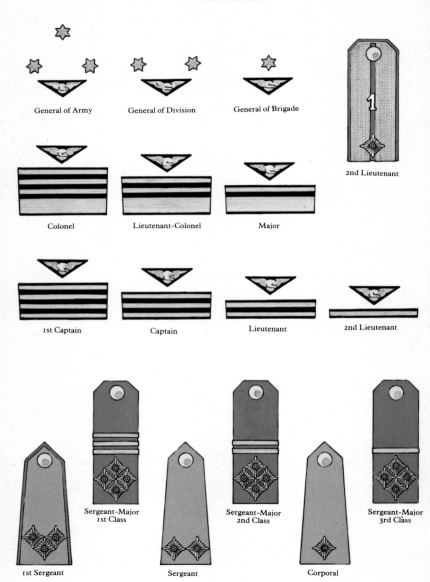

General of Army

General of Division

General of Brigade

2nd Lieutenant

Colonel

Lieutenant-Colonel

Major

1st Captain

Captain

Lieutenant

2nd Lieutenant

1st Sergeant

Sergeant-Major 1st Class

Sergeant

Sergeant-Major 2nd Class

Corporal

Sergeant-Major 3rd Class

PLATE 28

HISTORICAL BACKGROUND

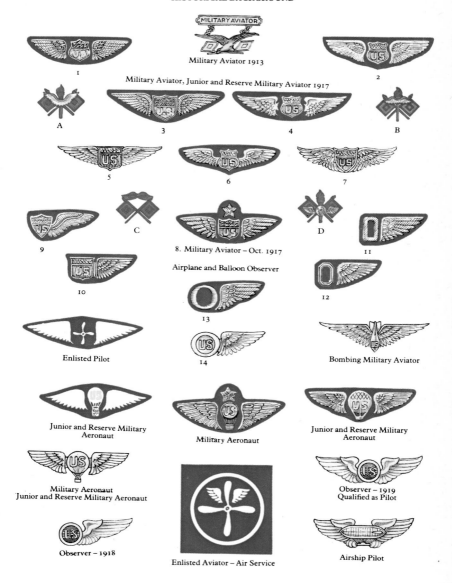

Military Aviator 1913

I

2

Military Aviator, Junior and Reserve Military Aviator 1917

A

3

4

B

5

6

7

C

9

8. Military Aviator – Oct. 1917

D

10

11

Airplane and Balloon Observer

12

13

Enlisted Pilot

14

Bombing Military Aviator

Junior and Reserve Military
Aeronaut

Military Aeronaut

Junior and Reserve Military
Aeronaut

Military Aeronaut
Junior and Reserve Military Aeronaut

Observer – 1919
Qualified as Pilot

Observer – 1918

Enlisted Aviator – Air Service

Airship Pilot

PLATE 29

CAP BADGES AND OTHER INSIGNIA

Cadets
U.S.A.A.F.

Officers
U.S.A.A.F.

Enlisted Men
U.S.A.A.F.

Officers' Collar Badges
U.S.A.A.F.

Warrant/Flight Officer
U.S.A.A.F.

Enlisted Men's Collar Badges
U.S.A.A.F.

Warrant Officer
U.S. Navy Aviation

Officers/Chief W.O.
U.S. Navy Aviation

Petty Officers
U.S. Navy Aviation

U.S. Navy Aviators
(Garrison Cap)

U.S.M.C. Aviation Cadets
Garrison Cap

Petty Officers
U.S.C.G. Aviation

Officers
U.S.C.G. Aviation

Warrant Officers
U.S.C.G. Aviation

Officers
Collar – right

Officers (Dress)
U.S.M.C. Aviation

Enlisted Men
U.S.C.G. Aviation

Enlisted Men
Garrison Cap

Enlisted Men (Dress)
U.S.M.C. Aviation

PLATE 30

OFFICERS' AND WARRANT OFFICERS' RANK INSIGNIA

General

Lieutenant General

Major General

Brigadier General

Vice Admiral
U.S.N./U.S.C.G.

Colonel

Lieutenant Colonel

Major General
U.S.M.C.

Major

Captain

1st Lieutenant

2nd Lieutenant

Colonel
U.S.A.A.F.

Chief Warrant Officer

Flight Officer

Warrant Officer
Junior Grade

Flight Officer
U.S.A.A.F.

Chief W.O.

Commissioned W.O.

W.O.

Lieutenant
U.S.N./U.S.C.G.

Chief W.O.s' and W.O.s' Sleeve Stripes

2nd Lieutenant
U.S.M.C.

PLATE 31

ARMY AVIATION N.C.O.s' RANK BADGES

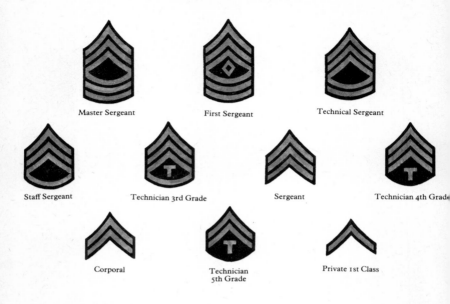

Master Sergeant

First Sergeant

Technical Sergeant

Staff Sergeant

Technician 3rd Grade

Sergeant

Technician 4th Grade

Corporal

Technician
5th Grade

Private 1st Class

ARMY AVIATION CADETS' RANK BADGES

Battalion
Commander

Company
Commander

Lieutenant

Battalion Adjutant

Color Sergeant

First Sergeant

Battalion
Sergeant Major

Supply Sergeant

Sergeant

Color Corporal

Corporal

PLATE 32

ARMY AVIATION CADETS' RANK BADGES – OVERCOAT

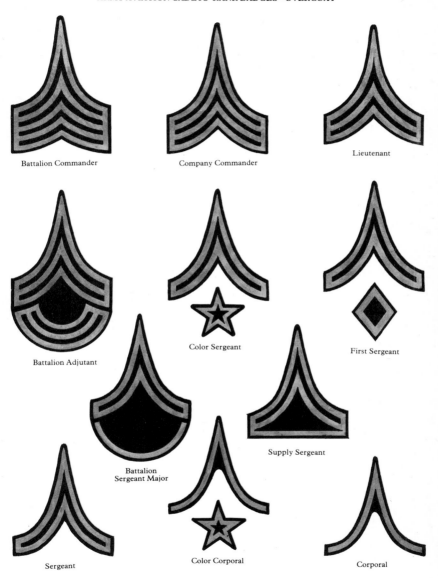

Battalion Commander

Company Commander

Lieutenant

Battalion Adjutant

Color Sergeant

First Sergeant

Battalion
Sergeant Major

Supply Sergeant

Sergeant

Color Corporal

Corporal

PLATE 33

PETTY OFFICERS' RATINGS – U.S. NAVY AND COAST GUARD

Chief Petty Officer
Aviation Metalsmith

Chief Petty Officer
Av. Electrician's Mate
12 years with Good Conduct

Petty Officer 2nd Class
Av. Radioman

Petty Officer 3rd Class
Av. General Utility

Petty Officer 1st Class
Av. Machinist's Mate
8 years Service

Seaman/Fireman
1st Class

Seaman/Fireman
2nd Class

Apprentice Seaman/Fireman
3rd Class

Lieutenant Junior Grade

(Winter Working Coat)

(Dress and Blue Service Coat)

Aviation Cadet
U.S. Navy

Aviation Cadet
U.S.M.C.

U.S. Coast Guard shields, for Officers and W.O.s, Chief Petty Officer
and Enlisted Men, for winter and summer uniforms

PLATE 34

N.C.O.s' RANK BADGES – U.S. MARINE CORPS

First Sergeant

1st Grade Line

Band Leader

1st Grade Staff

2nd Grade Line

2nd Grade Staff

3rd Grade Line

3rd Grade Staff

4th Grade

5th Grade

6th Grade

Enlistment Stripes

1st Class Private
Musician

CIVIL AIR PATROL

Collar Badge

Cap Badge

Collar Badge

Pilot

Garrison Cap Badge

Duck Club

Observer

PLATES 35

QUALIFICATION BADGES

Command Pilot

Senior Pilot

Pilot

Balloon Pilot

Senior Balloon Pilot

Balloon Observer

Aircraft Observer

Technical Observer

Navigator

Bombardier

Aerial Gunner

Air Crew Member

Glider Pilot

Service Pilot

Liaison Pilot

Women's Air Force
Service Pilot

Flight Surgeon
1st type

Women's Army
Service Pilot

Flight Nurse
1st type

Flight Surgeon
2nd type

Flight Nurse
2nd type

Pilot
U.S.N./U.S.M.C./U.S.C.G.

Observer
U.S.N./U.S.M.C.

Balloon Pilot
U.S.N./U.S.M.C.

Naval Combat Air Crew
Member

Flying Instructor

Flight Surgeon
U.S.N./U.S.M.C./U.S.C.G.

PLATE 36

NAVAL SPECIALITY AND DISTINGUISHING MARKS

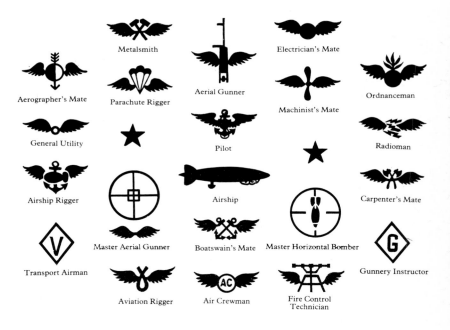

Metalsmith

Aerographer's Mate

Parachute Rigger

Aerial Gunner

Electrician's Mate

Machinist's Mate

Ordnanceman

General Utility

Pilot

Radioman

Airship Rigger

Master Aerial Gunner

Airship

Master Horizontal Bomber

Carpenter's Mate

Transport Airman

Boatswain's Mate

Gunnery Instructor

Aviation Rigger

Air Crewman

Fire Control Technician

AIR CARRIER CONTRACT PERSONNEL – A.T.C., U.S.A.A.F.

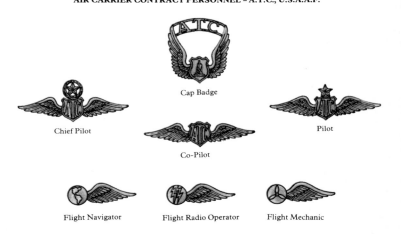

Cap Badge

Chief Pilot

Co-Pilot

Pilot

Flight Navigator

Flight Radio Operator

Flight Mechanic

PLATE 37

U.S.A.

U.S. ARMY AIR FORCES' SHOULDER SLEEVE INSIGNIA

U.S.A.A.F.
Instructor

U.S. Army Air Forces
1st and 2nd type

1st Air Force

2nd Air Force

3rd Air Force

4th Air Force

5th Air Force

6th Air Force

7th Air Force

8th Air Force

9th Air Force

10th Air Force

11th Air Force

12th Air Force

13th Air Force

14th Air Force

15th Air Force

20th Air Force

Mediterranean Allied
Air Force

Strategic Air Force

Airborne Troop
Carrier

Desert Air Force

SPECIALISTS' CUFF INSIGNIA

Engineering
Specialist

Armature
Specialist

Photography
Specialist

Communication
Specialist

Weather
Specialist

Air Force Cadet

Air Force Cadet

PLATE 38

U.S. MARINE CORPS, CIVIL AIR PATROL, ETC. SHOULDER SLEEVE AND CUFF INSIGNIA

HQ, U.S.M.C.
Air Force – Pacific

U.S.M.C. Aircraft
1st Wing

U.S.M.C. Aircraft
2nd Wing

U.S.M.C. Aircraft
3rd Wing

U.S.M.C. Aircraft
4th Wing

Air Transport
Command

HQ Pacific
Aircraft Wing

High School Victory
Corps – Air

Aircraft F.M.F.
2nd Wing

Aircraft F.M.F.
3rd Wing

Aircraft F.M.F.
1st Wing

Aircraft F.M.F.
4th Wing

1st Marine Amphibious Corps
Aviation Engineers

Air Transport Command
Ground Personnel

Women's Ferrying Command

Coastal
Patrol

Civil Air Patrol

Civil Air Patrol
Cadet

Civil Air Patrol
Guard

Photography

Liaison
Patrol

Forest
Patrol

Courier
Service

Transportation

Radio

Band

PLATE 39

HISTORICAL BACKGROUND

Artillery Aviation
Shoulder Strap's Title

87th Squadron
Shoulder Strap's Title

Pilot
W.W.I

Aviation – Aircraft
1915–23

Observer
W.W.I

Balloon Observer
W.W.I

Machine-Gunner
W.W.I

Pilot

Aviation-Airship

Mechanic

Pilot
1923–35

Balloon Engineers
1931

Observer
1931

Ballon Observer
1931

Observer

Airship Commander

Airship 2nd Officer

Airship Crew Officer

Ex-war Pilot
Army

1,000,000 Km Award
Civil Aviation

Bailoon Battalions

PLATE 40

CAP INSIGNIA

Generals
General of Air Brigade

Generals
Aviation Engineers

Officers
Specialists' Role – Fitter

A.E. Technical
Assistants Role

Senior Officers
Lieutenant-Colonel

C.C. Commissariat
Role

Services Role

C.C. Administrative
Role

Junior Officers
Lieutenant

Medical Corps

Flying Role

Forage Cap Badge
Gold Embroidered

Warrant Officers
All W.O.s' ranks

Forage Cap Badge
Yellow machine-embroidered

Forage Cap Badge
Yellow hand-embroidered

Chaplains

Forage Cap Badge
Yellow hand-embroidered

PLATE 41

OFFICERS' RANK BADGES – SERVICE UNIFORM

Air Marshal and Generals

Air Marshal

General of Air Army

Generals
Services Role

General of Air Squad
in command of Air Army

General of Air Squad

General of Air Division

General of Air Brigade

Senior Officer
Flying Role

Colonel

Lieutenant-Colonel

Major

Senior Officer
Medical Corps

Junior Officer
A.E. Engineers Role

Captain

Lieutenant

2nd Lieutenant

Junior Officer
C.C. Commissariat Role

Junior Officer
S.R. Photographer

Captain
A.E.Engineers Role

Captain
C.C. Commissariat Role

Junior Officer
Chaplain

PLATE 42

OFFICERS' SHOULDER BOARDS FOR FULL DRESS UNIFORM

General
of Air Squad

Lieutenant-General
C.C. Commissariat Role

Major
A.E. Engineers Role

Captain
S.R. Fitter

Captain
Chaplain

OFFICERS' SHOULDER BOARDS FOR COLONIAL AND OTHER UNIFORMS

**W.O.s/SERGEANTS
FULL DRESS UNIFORM**

**CORPORALS/AIRMEN
FULL DRESS UNIFORM**

General of Air Brigade
Medical Corps

Colonel
Flying Role

Lieutenant
C.C. Administrative Role

Chief W.O.
Flying Role

Airman
S.R. Electrician

WARRANT OFFICERS' AND N.C.O.s' RANK BADGES

Aiutante di battaglia
S.R.Radio-Aerologist

W.O. Major
Bandsman

Chief W.O.
Flying Role

W.O.
A.E. Technical Assistant

Sergeant-Major

Sergeant

First Airman

Leading Airman

PLATE 43

QUALIFICATION BADGES

Pilot

Observer

Observer

Pilot
Velocity

Pilot
Stratosphere

Pilot
Atlantic

Air Crew Member

Torpedo Aircraft
Crew Member

Interceptors

Bombers

Torpedo Aircraft

Assault-Combat

Reconnaissance
at Sea

Strategic
Reconnaissance

Diver Aircraft

Transport

Rescue

Aerial Observation

Fitter

A.F. Parachutist
1942–45

Electro-mechanic

Motorist

Photographer

Armourer

PLATE 44

ARM-OF-SERVICE (CATEGORY) BADGES

Photographer | Armourer | Electrician | Driver | Mechanic | Fitter | Radio-Aerologist

Fitter Instruments | Technical Assistant | Medical Orderly | Wireless Operator | Troops Admin. Service

ARM BADGES AND MISCELLANEA

Air Force in the Aegean

1st Interceptors Group

Assault Pilot | Bandmaster | Fencing Instructor

★ REGIA AERONAUTICA ★

Tally for Summer Hat

THE AIR FORCE OF THE ITALIAN SOCIAL REPUBLIC

Generals' National Insignia

Officers' and Airmens' Cap Badges

All Other Ranks' National Insignia

Torpedo Aircraft

Interceptors

Torpedo Aircraft

PLATE 45

CAP AND OTHER BADGES

Officers

Privates

N.C.O.s

OFFICERS' RANK BADGES

Collar Badges

General

Lieutenant-General

Major-General

General Staff Academy

Colonel

Lieutenant-Colonel

Major

General Staff Academy
Collar Badges

Captain

1st Lieutenant

2nd Lieutenant

Corporal – A.A. School

PLATE 46

CAP, COLLAR AND RANK BADGES

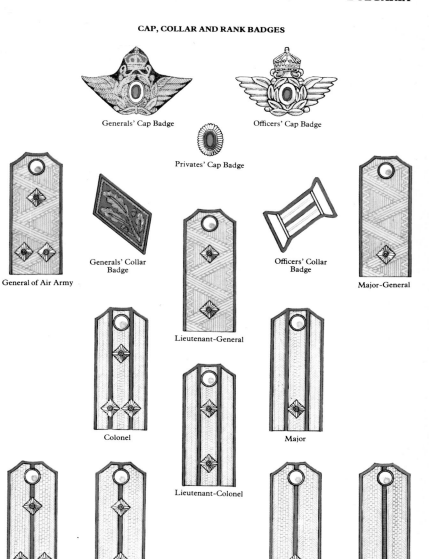

Generals' Cap Badge

Officers' Cap Badge

Privates' Cap Badge

General of Air Army

Generals' Collar Badge

Officers' Collar Badge

Major-General

Lieutenant-General

Colonel

Major

Lieutenant-Colonel

Captain

1st Lieutenant

2nd Lieutenant

Candidate Officer

PLATE 47

BULGARIA

N.C.O.s' RANK BADGES

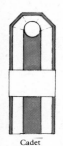
Cadet

Sergeant-Major

Sergeant

Candidate Sergeant

Corporal

GERMANY

HISTORICAL BACKGROUND

Pilot

Observer
(Bavarian)

Observer

Naval Pilot
(Sea)

Aviator
Commemorative Badge

Naval Pilot
(Land)

Airship Crew (Navy)
Commemorative Badge

Naval Observer

Air Gunner

Naval Pilot
Commemorative Badge

Airship Crew (Army)
Commemorative Badge

Naval Observer
Commemorative Badge

PLATE 48

CAP INSIGNIA

Reichsmarschall of Great Germany

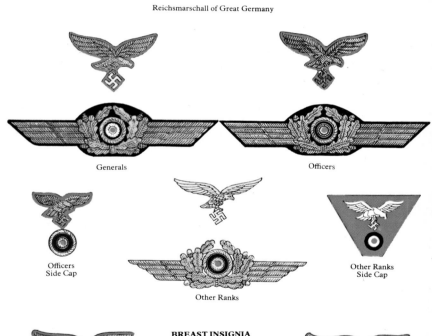

Generals

Officers

Officers
Side Cap

Other Ranks

Other Ranks
Side Cap

BREAST INSIGNIA

Generals

Other Ranks

Officers

PLATE 49

FIELD-MARSHALS' AND GENERALS' RANK INSIGNIA

Reichsmarschall of Great Germany
1st type

2nd type

Field-Marshal .

Colonel-General

Lieutenant-General
(Officials)

General of Aviation

Lieutenant-General

Major-General

Major-General
(Medical Corps)

PLATE 50

OFFICERS' RANK INSIGNIA

1st Lieutenant
(Flyer Reserve)

Senior Inspector
(Officials)

Colonel
(General Staff)

Lieutenant-Colonel
(Air Ministry)

Major
(Flyer)
Retired List

Captain Re-enlisted
(Flyer)

Captain
(Anti-Aircraft)

1st Lieutenant
(Signals)

Lieutenant
(Medical)

1st Lieutenant
(General Göring)

Officers' Collar Patches of the H. Göring Tank Division
1st and 2nd Pattern

PLATE 51

N.C.O.s' RANK BADGES

Stabsfeldwebel
(Flyer)

Oberfeldwebel
(H. Göring Tank Div.)

Wachtmeister
(A.A. Artillery)

Unterfeldwebel
(Medical Corps)

Unteroffizier
(Construction Troops)
after 1939

Stabsgefreiter
N.C.O. Candidate
(Jäger Bn H. Göring)

Obergefreiter
(Signals)

Gefreiter
(Air Traffic Control)

Flieger
(Flying Troops)

Stabsgefreiter
after 1944

Hauptgefreiter
until 1944

Obergefreiter

Gefreiter

PLATE 52

RANK BADGES FOR FLYING FIELD/UNIFORMS

Field-Marshal

Colonel-General

General of Aviation

Lieutenant-General

Major-General

1st Lieutenant
(Corps of Administrative
Officials)

Colonel

Lieutenant-Colonel

Major

Captain

1st Lieutenant

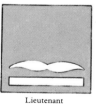

Lieutenant

Stabsfeldwebel

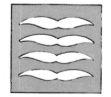

Oberfeldwebel

Feldwebel

Unterfeldwebel

Unteroffizier

PLATE 53

GERMANY

ENGINEERING CORPS' RANK INSIGNIA

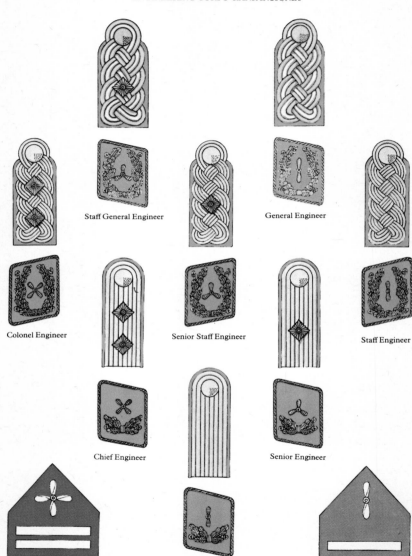

Staff General Engineer

General Engineer

Colonel Engineer

Senior Staff Engineer

Staff Engineer

Chief Engineer

Senior Engineer

Colonel Engineer

Engineer

Engineer

PLATE 54

MUSICIANS' RANK INSIGNIA

Music-Superintendent
1935–38

Note: Arm-of-service
colour refers to the
branch of service

Staff Music-Master
1935–38

Senior Music-Master
1935–38

Music-Master
1935–38

All three ranks
1935–38
(Flying Troops)

Senior Music-Superintendent
1938–39

Music-Superintendent
1938–39

Senior Music-Superintendent
1939–45

Music-Superintendent
1939–45

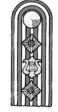

Staff Music-Master
1938–45

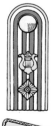

Senior Music-Master
1938–45

Music Master
1938–45

Music-Leader

Musician

PLATE 55

CUFF TITLES

Jagdgeschwader Richthofen

Geschwader General Wever

Geschwader Horst Wessel

Geschwader Immelmann

Jagdgeschwader Mölders

Geschwader Hindenburg

Geschwader Boelcke

Jagdgeschwader Udet

Legion Condor

Fallschirm-Division

Jagdgeschwader Schlageter

General Göring

HERMANN GÖRING

Hermann Göring

AFRIKA

Fallschirm-Jäger Rgt. 1 .2

PLATE 56

COMMEMORATIVE CUFF TITLES

Jagdgeschwader 1917/18
Frhr. v. Richthofen Nr.1

Jagdstaffel 1916/18
Boelcke Nr.2

QUALIFICATION BADGES AND AWARDS

Air Crew

Pilot

Observer

Pilot-Observer

Air Gunner
Flight Engineer

Glider Pilot

Wireless Operator
Air Gunner

Parachutist

Ex-Flyer

Un-qualified
Air Gunner

A.A. Artillery
Award

Ground-Combat
Award

100 Ground-Combat
Engagements Award

Sea Battle
Award

Tank Battle
Award

75 Tank Battle
Engagements Award

PLATE 57

QUALIFICATION CLASPS

Long-Range Fighters and Air-to-Ground Support Aircraft

Day Interceptors

Night Long-Range Fighters and Night Intruder Aircraft

Bombers

Night Interceptors

Reconnaissance

Transport and Gliders

Ground Combat

Air-to-Ground Support

SPECIALITY AND TRADE BADGES AND AWARDS

Technical Aviation Personnel

Flying Personnel

Anti-Aircraft Personnel

Signaller not in Signal Unit

Armourer N.C.O.

Armourer N.C.O. Flying and Signal Units

Administrative N.C.O.

Ordnance

Teletype N.C.O.

Teletype Operator

Transport N.C.O.

Qualified Telephonist N.C.O.

Qualified Telephone Operator

Qualified Radio N.C.O.

Qualified Radioman

Qualified Sound Location N.C.O.

Qualified Sound Location Operator

PLATE 58

SPECIALITY AND TRADE BADGES

Radio Direction
N.C.O.

Radio Direction
Finder

Mechanised Transport
Equipment Administrator
Candidate

A.A. Artillery

Signal Equipment
Administrator

Searchlight Equipment
Administrator

Medical Orderly

Military Boats
Personnel

'C' Qualified
Radioman A.A.

Master Radioman

Air Raid Warning
Personnel

Aircraft Equipment
Administrator

Driver

Technical Preparatory
School Graduate

N.C.O.s' School

Armourer
Light Bombs

Technical N.C.O.

Armourer
Heavy Bombs

Farrier

Sound Locator Crewman
(1 year service)

Range-Finder Crewman
(1 year service)

Sound Locator Crewman

Standard Bearer

Range-Finder Crewman

PLATE 59

CZECHOSLOVAKIA

CAP BADGES

Officers
(Non-combatant)

N.C.O.s
(Combatant)

Other Ranks

RANK BADGES

Generals
(Stars on sleeves)

Colonel

Lieutenant-Colonel

Major

Staff Captain

Captain

Senior Lieutenant

Lieutenant

Junior Lieutenant

Warrant Officer 1930–38
(3 Ranks)

Staff Warrant Officer post–1938

PLATE 60

RANK BADGES

Warrant Officer

Staff Sergeant

Sergeant

Senior Platoon Sergeant

Platoon Sergeant

Corporal

Lance Corporal

QUALIFICATION BADGES

Army Observer

Air Gunner

Pilot

Observer

Observer
(Balloon)

Officer attached to R.A.F.V.R.

Pilot
(Balloon)

PLATE 61

FINLAND

CAP BADGES

Officers'
Peaked cap

1

2

3

4

OFFICERS' RANK BADGES

Lieutenant-General

Major-General

QUALIFICATION BADGE

Pilot

OFFICERS OF THE SERVICES

Colonel

Lieutenant-Colonel

Major

Lieutenant-Colonel
Doctor

Captain

Lieutenant

2nd Lieutenant

Lieutenant
Technician

PLATE 62

N.C.O.s' RANK BADGES

Flight Sergeant

Senior Sergeant

Sergeant

Junior Sergeant

Corporal

Arm-of-service Badge

Airman

POLAND

HISTORICAL BACKGROUND

Aviation in
Greater Poland

Aviation in
France

Shoulder Straps
Badge

Krakow Pilots' School

1917

1919

7th Kościuszko
Air Squadron

Flyers' Arm Badge
Aircraft

Military Aviation
Courses

Doctor

Air Gunner

Photographer/ Surveyor

PLATE 63

CAP BADGES (1936)

General
of Brigade

Officers/W.O.

Lieutenant-Colonel

Captain

Generals

Warrant Officer

Senior Officers   Junior Officers

Lance Sergeant

Sergeant

**OTHER RANKS' CAP BADGE
AND CAP BAND RANK INSIGNIA**

Staff Sergeant

Sergeant

Lance Sergeant

Corporal

Lance Corporal

PLATE 64

OFFICERS' RANK BADGES

Generals

General

General of Division

General of Brigade

General Staff

Bandmaster

Bandsman

Catholic Chaplain

Protestant Chaplain

Orthodox Chaplain

Colonel

Lieutenant-Colonel

Major

N.C.O.s' School

Cadet (Regular)

Cadet (Regular)

Captain

Lieutenant

2nd Lieutenant

Cadet (Reserve)

Cadet (Reserve)

PLATE 65

WARRANT OFFICERS' AND N.C.O.s' RANK BADGES AND MISCELLANEA

Warrant Officer

Staff Sergeant

Sergeant

Lance Sergeant

Corporal

Lance Corporal

Officers' Dress Belt

Examples of Officers' and N.C.O.s' Badges for Flying Uniform

Voluntary Training Flights – Examples of Officers' and N.C.O.s' armlets

PLATE 66

CAP BADGES WORN AFTER 1939

Officers/W.O.

All Ranks
Forage cap

Other Ranks

Generals   Colonel

SHOULDER FLASHES (AFTER 1939)

Airmen

Airmen

Officers

Polish Volunteers from France, Belgium, North and South America

PLATE 67

POLAND

OFFICERS' RANK BADGES (AFTER 1939)

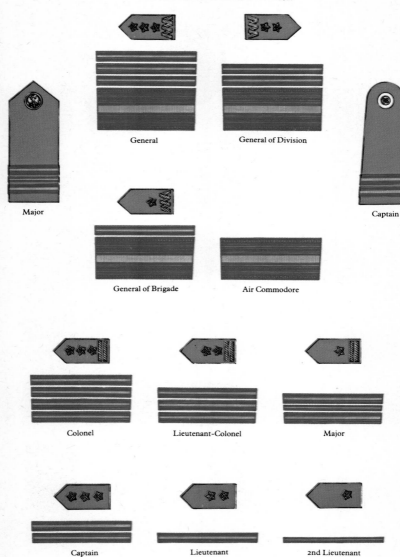

General

General of Division

Major

Captain

General of Brigade

Air Commodore

Colonel

Lieutenant-Colonel

Major

Captain

Lieutenant

2nd Lieutenant

PLATE 68

WARRANT OFFICERS' AND N.C.O.s' RANK BADGES (AFTER 1939)

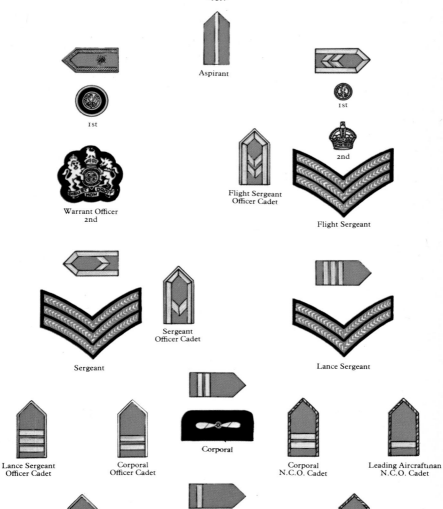

Aspirant

1st

1st

2nd

Warrant Officer
2nd

Flight Sergeant
Officer Cadet

Flight Sergeant

Sergeant
Officer Cadet

Sergeant

Lance Sergeant

Corporal

Lance Sergeant
Officer Cadet

Corporal
Officer Cadet

Corporal
N.C.O. Cadet

Leading Aircraftman
N.C.O. Cadet

Leading Aircraftman

Leading Aircraftman
Officer Cadet

Aircraftman
N.C.O. Cadet

PLATE 69

QUALIFICATION BADGES

Pilot
1919/42/44

Pilot
1919/33

Pilot 1st Class
1933

Pilot 2nd Class
1933

Observer (Combat)
1919/33

Observer 1919/42/44
Observer 1st Class 1933

Observer 2nd Class
1933

Pilot-Observer
(Combat) 1928

Pilot-Observer
1928

Radio Observer
1942

Air Gunner – Radio Operator
1942

Air Gunner
1942

Flight Engineer
1942

PLATE 70

QUALIFICATION BADGES

Air Gunner – Radio Operator
1944

Air Gunner
1944

Flight Meteorologist
1944

Flight Engineer
1944

Bombardier
1944

Artillery Observer
Aircraft Pilot

Naval Aviation
Pilot 1st Class
1933

Airship Mechanics
1922

Naval Aviation
Pilot 2nd Class
1933

Naval Aviation
Observer 1st Class
1933

Balloon Observer
1st Class
1933

Naval Aviation
Observer 2nd Class
1933

Air Gunner 1st Class
1933

Balloon Observer
2nd Class
1933

Air Gunner 2nd Class
1933

PLATE 71

POLAND

QUALIFICATION BADGES

Specialist N.C.O. 1st Class
1933

Technical Officer 1st Class
1933

Doctor 1st Class
1933

Specialist N.C.O. 2nd Class
1933

Technical Officer 2nd Class
1933

Doctor 2nd Class
1933

OTHER BADGES

Staff College

Balloon Insignia

N.C.O.s' School

Officers' School

No. 55 Squadron

National Aircraft
Factory

1st Aviation Regt

2nd Aviation Regt

3rd Aviation Regt

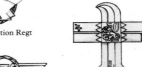

4th Aviation Regt

Air Defence League

5th Aviation Regt

6th Aviation Regt

Pilots' School

PLATE 72

SQUADRON BADGES

663rd A.O.P. Sq.

No. 300

No. 301

Polish Fighting Team

No. 302

No. 303

No. 304

No. 305

No. 306

No. 307

No. 308

No. 309

No. 315

No. 316

No. 317

No. 318

JAPAN

CAP BADGES OF ARMY AND NAVAL AVIATION

Officers

Officers

Other Ranks

Petty Officers

Ratings

Ratings

Ratings

PLATE 73

JAPAN

RANK BADGES

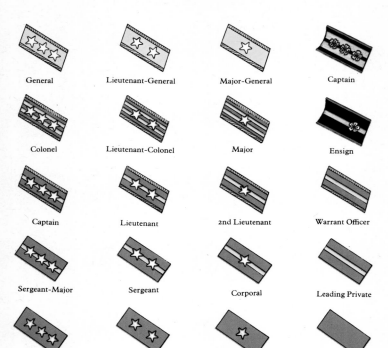

General	Lieutenant-General	Major-General	Captain
Colonel	Lieutenant-Colonel	Major	Ensign
Captain	Lieutenant	2nd Lieutenant	Warrant Officer
Sergeant-Major	Sergeant	Corporal	Leading Private
Superior Private	Private 1st Class	Private 2nd Class	Recruit

Commander

Vice Admiral

Lieutenant Commander

Ensign

PLATE 74

PETTY OFFICERS' AND SEAMENS' RANK BADGES

OTHER BADGES

Bomber Pilot

Senior Petty Officer

Petty Officer 1st Class

Petty Officer 2nd Class

Fighter Pilot

Leading Seaman

Senior Seaman

Seaman 1st Class

Aviation Badge

Pilot

Aviation Badge

Collar Badge

Army Aviation School

Collar Badge

Officers' Army Aviation
School

Army Aviation Maintenance School

22nd Army Air Kikusi
Squadron

3rd Army Aviation Squadron

Kumagai Army Aviation
School

PLATE 75

RUMANIA

RANK BADGES

General Inspector of the
Air Force

General of Air Squad

Commander

Captain Commander

Lieutenant Commander

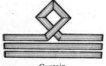

Captain

Lieutenant

2nd Lieutenant

Lieutenant
(Engineer)

Chief Warrant Officer   Warrant Officer Major

Warrant Officer   Junior Warrant Of

PLATE 76

RANK BADGES

Warrant Officer
(Ground Personnel)

Sergeant

Corporal

Private 1st Class

ARM-OF-SERVICE BADGES – COLLAR PATCHES

Generals

Physicians

Mechanics

Anti-Aircraft

Reconnaissance

Bombers

Fighters

Engineers

Aerostation

Schools

QUALIFICATION BADGES

Pilot

Pilot-Bomber

Observer

PLATE 77

HUNGARY

CAP INSIGNIA – PEAKED CAP

Officers

Other Ranks' Cap Badge

W.O./Sergeants

FORAGE CAP

Lieutenant-General

Major-General

Colonel

Lieutenant-Colonel

Major

Captain

1st Lieutenant

2nd Lieutenant

Candidate Officer

Warrant Officer

Senior Staff Sergeant

Staff Sergeant

Sergeant

Corporal-Major

Corporal

Senior Airman

PLATE 78

OFFICERS' RANK BADGES

Major-General
Flying Suit

Lieutenant-General

Major-General

Lieutenant-Colonel
'Flying Suit

Colonel

Lieutenant-Colonel
(General Staff)

Major

Captain

1st Lieutenant

2nd Lieutenant

QUALIFICATION BADGES

Officer Pilot

N.C.O. Pilot

PLATE 79

WARRANT OFFICERS' AND N.C.O.s'
RANK BADGES

Warrant Officer
Flying Suit

Aspirant

Warrant Officer

Senior Staff Sergeant
Flying Suit

Senior Staff Sergeant

Staff Sergeant

Sergeant

Corporal Major

Corporal

Senior Airman

Airman

Collar Badge

PLATE 80

Collar Badges

The first badge for medical officers was adopted in 1918 and resembles that of the Royal Army Medical Corps, except for the motto which in the case of the R.A.F. badge read 'Nec Aspera Terrent'. A smaller different badge was instituted two years later.

Gilt, silver and brass versions were worn by officers on service dress and mess dress and by orderlies, respectively. Later a different badge was worn by the personnel of the Dental Branch. Chaplains wore their distinctive badge, minus the crown, on the collar of the service and mess dress uniforms; in the case of Jewish chaplains the Cross Patee was replaced by the Star of David.

The Educational Officers of the R.A.F.V.R. obtained their own collar badges in 1940, above which were attached the 'VR' titles. There was also another title in existence: a plain letter 'A' for Auxiliary (Plate 4), and both titles were used in two sizes, for the jacket collar and a larger size for the greatcoat's shoulder straps, plus embroidered variations of both which were worn beneath the shoulder flash by N.C.O.s and airmen. The Auxiliary Air Force was formed in 1924 while the R.A.F. Volunteer Reserve was instituted in 1937.

Plate 3. Pilots' Wings

The first 'wings' were granted to qualified pilots in 1913 and when five years later the Royal Air Force was formed, the initials in the centre of the wings were changed from R.F.C. to R.A.F. It should be noted that the first wings depicted the R.F.C. badge, as worn on the cap and collar, with additional wings on either side. In 1918 the officers' cap badges were changed and collar badges were abolished (for exceptions see previous section), therefore since 1918 the centrepiece of the wings resembles the design of the cap badge of the airmen, who cannot qualify for the badge in any case.

A great number of variations of R.A.F. pilots' wings could be found: there were metal badges with a brooch pin at the back and others embroidered in gold and silver wire on the uniform's cloth, for full dress. Some other wings of the R.F.C. were embroidered in gold and silver on dark blue cloth and were worn on patrol tunics while smaller badges, also embroidered in metal wire were used for the mess dress.

The wings for service dress were embroidered in silk or cotton on a dark blue, or black cloth backing: some of these were flat while others had a padded base. The wings, crown and initials were usually executed with buff coloured cotton while the wreath was brown.

Wings of the same basic design were used in the Commonwealth but the centrepiece of the badge was different. The pilots' wings of the Royal Canadian Air Force had the initials R.C.A.F. in the centre while Australian pilots had the appropriate initials R.A.A.F. in the centre of their badge which was usually white with a light blue wreath.

The South African Air Force wings were made of white silk with a shield in the centre depicting the figure of Hope of the Cape Province, the 'wildebeeste' of Natal, the orange tree of the Orange Free State and the waggon of Transvaal. Early wings, made of brass, depicted the Union coat of arms below the crown, encircled by a wreath with the usual side wings (Plate 1).

The initials 'N.Z.' were present in the centre of the wings of the New Zealand Air Force.

Aircrew Badges—R.A.F.

These qualification badges are commonly known as 'half-wings' and as with the pilot's wings are worn above the left breast pocket, and above any ribbons or decorations.

The Observer's badge was adopted in September 1915 and was replaced in 1942 by the Navigator's badge as by then the functions of the Observer had been taken over by the more complex duties of the latter. The badge of the former depicted a wing with fourteen feathers protruding from an 'O'. The wing of the Navigator and the other aircrew's wings usually have twelve feathers only.

Another early qualification badge which has been illustrated among arm badges (Plate 6) is that of Air Gunner; it depicts a winged bullet, all made of brass. It was adopted in 1923 and in December 1939 was superseded by a half-wing with the letters 'A.G.' in the centre. Other aircrew qualification badges were adopted in 1942 and, in the following years, with their own appropriate initial or initials in the centre.

The Parachute Jumping Instructor badge was adopted shortly after World War 2 and this was the first time that the P.J.I.s were formally awarded aircrew status. It shows an open parachute in the centre instead of the usual initials.

These half-wings were all embroidered on dark blue or black backing cloth and, like the pilot's wings, there are flat and padded variations. A smaller, flat variation of these exists as well: this was usually worn by foreign aviators who had other badges on the breast as well.

Personnel of the Pathfinder squadrons, employed in finding and marking targets for oncoming bombers obtained their own distinctive badge in 1942. It was worn on the flap of the left breast pocket, 4.8 mm. below the seam. This was the eagle as worn on the forage cap, but in this case without the Royal Crown.

Aircrew Badges—R.C.A.F.

The Canadian aircrew members were eligible for the same qualifications as R.A.F. personnel but their badges were different. These half-wings carried the Royal Crown and the initials R.C.A.F. as well. However, the earlier Observer's badge was the usual winged 'O' which was granted during World War 1 to all Observers of the R.F.C. regardless of nationality.

Aircrew Badges—R.A.A.F.

The Australians had dark blue uniforms, therefore their aircrew badges were embroidered on bluish-grey felt, and the wreath was usually light blue, although variations exist which have all been embroidered in white.

Plate 4. Officers' Rank Badges

The R.A.F. officers' ranks that we know today were introduced on 27 August 1919 and new black and blue cuff stripes were adopted to be worn on the new grey-blue service dress. Gold stripes were worn on full dress and mess dress. Previously, khaki stripes were used on the war-time khaki uniform and gold stripes on the short lived sky blue uniforms.

The air force rank titles compare to the equivalent army ranks as follows:

Royal Air Force	Army
Marshal of the R.A.F.	Field-Marshal
Air Chief Marshal	General
Air Marshal	Lieutenant-General
Air Vice-Marshal	Major-General
Air Commodore	Brigadier-General
Group Captain	Colonel
Wing Commander	Lieutenant-Colonel
Squadron Leader	Major
Flight Lieutenant	Captain
Flying Officer	Lieutenant
Pilot Officer	2nd Lieutenant

The rank was shown by a combination of stripes of varying width: officers of Air Rank were distinguished by a wide stripe (2 inches) while the other officers had narrower stripes of two widths ($\frac{1}{2}$ inch and $\frac{1}{4}$ inch) appropriately combined.

On the greatcoat and on the blouse of the war-time grey-blue battle-dress the stripes were worn across the shoulder straps, as illustrated. The service dress jacket had no shoulder straps while the tunic of the full dress had shoulder straps with eagle and crown embroidered at the ends; officers of Air Rank wore an additional wreath embroidered in gold below the shoulder straps' button.

The women serving in the Women's Auxiliary Air Force had the same rank badges as the men but had different titles as shown in the following comparison chart:

W.A.A.F.	R.A.F.
Senior Controller	Air Commodore
Controller	Group Captain
Chief Commandant	Wing Commander
Senior Commandant	Squadron Leader
Company Commander	Flight Lieutenant
Deputy Company Commander	Flying Officer
Company Assistant	Pilot Officer

These rank titles were modelled after those of the A.T.S. but were changed in 1942 as follows:

W.A.A.F. 1st pattern	W.A.A.F. 2nd pattern
Senior Controller	Air Commandant
Controller	Group Officer
Chief Commandant	Wing Officer
Senior Commandant	Squadron Officer
Company Commander	Flight Officer
Deputy Company Commander	Section Officer
Company Assistant	Assistant Section Officer

Later the ranks of Commandant-in-Chief and Air Chief Commandant were also introduced, and compare with those of Air Marshal and Air Vice-Marshal respectively.

Plate 5. Warrant Officers' and N.C.O.s' Rank Badges

The warrant and non-commissioned ranks of the R.F.C. and later of the R.A.F. derive from those of the army, although some naval flavour is attached to the title of Leading Aircraftman.

The warrant ranks, of 1st and 2nd Class, existed until the beginning of World War 2: the former wore the Royal Arms on the forearm of both sleeves and the other a large Royal Crown, 45 × 45 mm. in size. The pre-war badges were usually embroidered in fine light blue silk, while later versions were embroidered in cotton on dark blue, or black felt. Eventually the two ranks were merged into one, of Warrant Officer, with the Royal Arms as its distinctive badge.

The Flight Sergeant was the top N.C.O.s' rank, with three worsted grey-blue chevrons and a crown above them. The latter was usually made of brass but light blue embroidered variations were used as well. Three- and two-chevron ranks identified the Sergeant and the Corporal while the army's one-chevron rank of Lance-Corporal was substituted by the two-bladed propeller badge of the Leading Aircraftman. The Leading Air-craftman, Aircraftman of 1st and of 2nd Class were graduation titles of airmen and the former became a rank title only in 1950 although the propeller badge existed since World War 1.

Four inverted 'V' chevrons below a drum were worn on the forearm by the Drum Major. Similar individual chevrons were also worn on the fore-arms and were known as good conduct stripes.

Initially the N.C.O.s' rank titles of the W.A.A.F. were different from those of the R.A.F.: there were Senior Section and Assistant Section Leaders, and Aircraftwomen of 1st and 2nd Class. Later the rank of Under Officer, equivalent to the R.A.F. Warrant Officer, was instituted and the women's rank titles were the same as those of the men.

Trade and Other Badges

Most of the following badges were worn on the sleeve and therefore have been illustrated together in this and in the following plates.

The eagle of the R.A.F. was worn on both upper sleeves, below the shoulder seam, by all those below the rank of Warrant Officer 1st Class; only the nationality title could be worn above the R.A.F. eagle. This badge was adopted in 1918 and was originally red for the khaki uniform of that period but subsequently its colour was changed to light blue when the grey-blue uniform was introduced. However, red eagles as well as other badges were worn on the khaki tropical uniforms of World War 2.

Airmen of the Royal Auxiliary Air Force and those of the Royal Air Force Volunteer Reserve wore the initials 'A' and 'VR' respectively, embroidered in light blue on dark blue background, immediately below the eagle badge.

The Warrant Officer wore the same badge below the rank badge. The same initials but made of brass were worn by the officers on the lapels of the service dress jacket and on the shoulder straps of the battledress and of the greatcoat (Plate 4). The letter 'A' was used also by personnel of the Women's Auxiliary Air Force. Later, during World War 2 the use of these initials was abandoned.

Bandsmen of the R.A.F. wore a brass badge depicting a lyre and wreath with the crown above, while musicians of voluntary bands had the same badge but without the crown. Trumpeters, pipers and drummers wore their own appropriate arm badges: crossed trumpets, a Scottish bagpipes and a drum, respectively.

The badge of Physical Training Instructor was already in use in the early 1920s and its original brass pattern was reproduced in cloth versions during World War 2 for reasons of economy. The remaining four badges illustrated in this plate were adopted during the last war: The Gunners were later taken over by the R.A.F. Regiment: the badge with two 'G's stands for Ground Gunner. The Parachute Instructor badge appeared in 1943 and was worn on the right upper sleeve as with that of Gunner, while the Signallers' badge was worn on both sleeves and was introduced in 1944 for qualified personnel of the R.A.F. Regiment.

Plate 6. Trade and Other Badges

The Combined Operations badge illustrated was worn by a member of the 3207 R.A.F. Servicing Command, one of several units with the new task of activating airstrips constructed by the Royal Engineers. These provisional airstrips, usually made of metal sheeting, were sited near the front line and were used as re-fuelling bases by fighter squadrons stationed in Britain. The Servicing Commando kept an airstrip going until the front line moved on and eventually passed its duty to normal R.A.F. units, before advancing to prepare another airstrip closer to the front line.

The Royal Air Force Regiment was raised in 1942 and was formed by ground personnel employed primarily in the defence of R.A.F. installations. All ranks wore a distinctive shoulder title on both upper arms.

Personnel engaged in Air-Sea Rescue wore a special badge on the right upper sleeve from 1943 to 1948.

Already, during World War 1, a special brass badge was created to distinguish Wireless Operators (Plate 1); the 'sparks' badge remained in use after the war and later the 'O' was replaced by a clenched fist, worn by Radio Operators and Mechanics, while Radio Operators had the initials 'RO' instead of the fist; other badges with different initials between the forks of lightning existed as well.

A brass badge, depicting a four-bladed propeller in a ring, was adopted in 1919 for boy apprentices and was worn on the left upper sleeve. The Air Gunner's badge was also made of brass: it has been mentioned already in the chapter on Aircrew badges.

The Bomb Disposal badge was adopted in 1941 for wearing on the right upper sleeve. The badge of the Eagle Squadron is a very exclusive item as it was worn from 1940 onward by Americans only, serving in that squadron. It was worn on both upper sleeves.

After dealing with each of these badges it becomes apparent that most pre-war badges were made of brass while war-time versions were later made in cloth purely for reasons of economy as thousands of men were by then wearing them. The cloth badges exist in embroidered and printed patterns, in light blue on dark blue background for grey-blue uniforms and red on khaki for khaki tropical uniforms.

The vast majority of the above-mentioned badges were used by N.C.O.s and airmen, therefore these had a dark blue or black background, while officers' badges were embroidered on a grey-blue background, to match the colour of the uniform.

Nationality Titles

During World War 2 the R.A.F. absorbed a number of servicemen from the Commonwealth and exiles from countries over-run by the enemy. The latter group is dealt with in their own national chapters in the book.

The colour of these nationality titles follows the general rule: the officers wore curved titles embroidered in light blue on grey-blue background, while the others had titles in light blue on dark blue or black background which was usually rectangular. All ranks wore red and khaki shoulder titles on the tropical uniform.

However, many badges that did not follow the rule were also made because many manufacturers were engaged in making these titles and they tried to improve on the average standard. In many instances the R.A.F. eagle and the nationality title were combined in the same badge, and different styles of lettering were applied. For instance, there are titles depicting the eagle above the initials U.S.A., others with 'CANADA' above the eagle and others with both national titles and the eagle in between. On the other hand, British airmen serving in Canada started wearing the 'GT. BRITAIN' title, and others appeared—i.e. the title 'SCOTLAND'.

All commonwealth nations, colonies and British territories were represented in this form and only a very few examples can be illustrated. Some other odd shoulder titles can be found as well, for instance that of 'MEXICO', probably worn by ex-residents in other nations.

Plate 7. Badges of Other Flying Organisations

Some extra-ordinary organisations were created during the years of national danger, giving a chance to many thousands to contribute in the cause of common defence. Only some representative badges of these organisations have been illustrated.

The Air Defence Cadet Corps was raised in 1938 to provide preliminary aviation training. The usual grey-blue R.A.F. uniforms were worn, with silver lace rank stripes. The officers' cap badge has been illustrated, the badge of cadets did not carry the wreath.

The Air Transport Auxiliary was an organisation employed in ferrying aircraft and general transportation. Many of the pilots were women. Dark blue uniforms were worn by its personnel with gold stripes on the cuffs, in a background in branch colour. The cap badge is illustrated but another variation existed, made of metal, with a scroll inscribed 'Aetheris Avidi'. Wings, half-wings and arm badges were worn as well by qualified personnel.

The personnel of the Civil Air Guard also had special badges; the pilots' wings depicted the initials as in the cap badge sided by straight wings. The Air Training Corps was created with the cadre of the Air Defence Cadet Corps in 1941. R.A.F. uniforms were used with R.A.F. stripes and chevrons and additional A.D.C. badges. The officers wore the 'VR' initials of the R.A.F. Volunteer Reserve in which they were commissioned.

Soon after it was raised, the Observer Corps was granted the prefix 'Royal' for its magnificent performance. The badge depicts an Elizabethan Coast Watcher, holding a torch above the motto 'Forewarned is Forearmed', surrounded by a wreath and ensigned by the Royal crown. The officers wore the initials 'ROC' on the lapels of the collar. The other ranks had an embroidered breast badge which, in a ring surmounted by the crown, shows the R.A.F. eagle surrounded by the title 'Royal Observer Corps'.

Fleet Air Arm Insignia

The Fleet Air Arm was formed in 1924 as a subordinate organisation to the R.A.F. and the seaborne contingent of the Fleet Air Arm came under the command of the Royal Navy in 1937 only.

Naval uniforms were worn by its personnel, with naval cap badges and rank insignia. In 1925 qualified pilots were granted a gold and silver embroidered badge which was worn on the left forearm above the rank stripes. The badge depicted an anchor surrounded by a wreath, below the Royal Crown, with an albatross wing on each side. A metal variation of this badge has been worn since 1933 on the breast on the white uniform only. R.A.F. officers attached to the Fleet Air Arm wore a similar badge but with out crown and wings.

Pilots who were recruited before the beginning of the war and did not belong to the naval establishment, therefore could not command H.M. vessels and were given a special badge — a silver 'A' surrounded by a gold wreath, which they wore above the rank insignia on the left sleeve. In 1939 a small letter 'A' was adopted in its place, worn inside the curl of the top stripe of both sleeves. The latter badge, however, was also worn by other officers of the Air Branch with qualifications other than that of pilot.

In 1942 a special arm badge was introduced for the Observers of the Fleet Air Arm: Air Gunners wore a similar badge and so, later, did other Aircrewmen ratings. These were embroidered in red for blue uniforms and in blue for white uniform, with or without crown.

Plate 8. Non-substantive Badges

These badges indentified the qualification, or specialisation of petty officers and seamen of the Royal Navy. The chief petty officers wore them in pairs, embroidered in gold on the lapels of the collar while larger badges, red for blue uniform and blue for white uniform were worn on the right arm by the other ratings. Gold badges were worn on full dress.

In 1930 the Telegraphist-Air Gunners of the Fleet Air Arm were granted a special badge which depicts an aeroplane with straight wings (Plate 7). Later, in 1935, a similar badge but with a 6-pointed star above the aeroplane was given to Air Gunners; a similar badge but with a crown instead of the star to Acting Observer's Mates, while the Observer's Mates had the aeroplane with the crown above and the star below.

These qualifications were reorganised in 1939 and the design of the aeroplane was also modified, as illustrated. The Air Mechanic qualification was instituted in the same year and that of Air Fitter in 1940. The badge of the former was a 2-bladed propeller while fitters wore a 4-bladed propeller. There were four sections of each of these qualifications: Airframe, Engine, Electrical and Ordnance.

The Chief Petty Officer Air Mechanic wore a crown above the propeller and a letter below referred to the section of specialisation. The leading ratings wore a star above the propeller and the letter, while the other ratings had the propeller and the letter only.

The crown was not worn with any of the fitters' badges. Unclassified badges, i.e. without the section's letter, were worn after 1943 by Air Mechanics and Fitters not yet qualified.

The Radio Mechanics of the Fleet Air Arm used the badge of the Royal Navy.

Norway

Plate 9. Cap Badges, Rank and Other Badges

At the outbreak of World War 2 Norway had a small Army Air Force and a Naval Air Service, both in existence since 1915. The aviators wore army or navy uniforms respectively, with additional qualification wings.

The army uniforms were modified in 1934 and the colour of piping and chevrons was changed from red to green. The officers' service dress consisted of a kepi or forage cap, a tunic with high folded collar and four patch pockets of usual pattern, Sam Browne belt, breeches and riding boots or long trousers and shoes. Double-breasted greatcoats and fur hats were used in winter. The other ranks wore the forage cap, a field-grey tunic with four patch pockets, a leather waist belt with a plain rectangular buckle, long trousers and boots. The buttons were shown on the greatcoat only.

A dual-badge was worn on the head-dress by officers and N.C.O.s, with stripes of gold, silver or black lace to identify class of rank. The officers had a silk cockade in the national colours at the top while that of the other ranks was made of metal and painted blue, white and red. The national emblem, the Norwegian Lion, was carried on the badge placed below by the officers, and on an arm-of-service button by the N.C.O.s. The officers' badge was made of gilt and enamel and was semi-spherical in shape. The privates wore the cockade only at the front of the forage cap.

Rank distinction was shown on the kepi, on the collar of the tunic and on the shoulder straps of the greatcoat or, in the case of N.C.O.s, on the cuffs.

Rank stripes were worn all around the kepi, above the chin strap. They were made of gold for generals and silver lace for the other officers; the former had also a special chin strap made of gold cords. The senior officers were identified by a large silver stripe with narrower rank stripes below while the lower three ranks had only the narrow stripes. The sergeants had narrow double green stripes placed vertically on the sides and on the back of the kepi, above the cap band. The Corporal wore single stripes in the same position.

There were two generals' ranks in 1940: the rank of General with three silver stars and of Major-General with one star only. A Colonel commanded the Army Air Force until 1924, later a Major-General.

Green piping was worn on the kepi, on the collar of the tunic, as illustrated, on the cuffs and on the shoulder straps of the greatcoat.

The generals had a large gold lace stripe at the front of the collar of the tunic, with large stars embroidered in silver thread. The senior officers had a silver stripe, 15 mm. wide, at the front of the collar and white metal 5-pointed stars identified the actual rank. Only the stars were worn by the junior officers, as illustrated.

These Norwegian officers' stars could be readily identified as at the end of each arm they have a small round loop which is used for stitching on to the uniform.

The stars and the senior officers' stripe were applied on the greatcoat's shoulder straps as well. The latter was stitched next to the outer green piping, all around the strap, except for the outer end that was attached to the shoulder seam.

The Sergeant wore one green stripe below the cuff piping of the tunic and the Corporal had a vertical green stripe on the cuff of both sleeves.

Wings were worn by qualified Pilots and Observers above the right breast pocket of the tunic. Both were embroidered in silver on a background of arm-of-service colour: red before 1934 and green from 1934 to 1940. Double wings, surmounted by the national coat of arms, were worn by Pilots while a half-wing, the Norwegian Lion in a shield below the crown was the badge of the Observers; both badges were instituted in February 1926. Naval aviators wore uniforms and badges of the Navy with the above-mentioned wings, embroidered in gold on dark blue background.

Plate 10. Badges worn after 1940

After the German invasion of Norway, in the spring of 1940, King Haakon VII and his government left for Britain where subsequently the Norwegian armed forces and the merchant marine were reorganised. At that time the Norwegian merchant marine was then the fourth largest in the world and as the majority of it joined the Allied cause, eventually it provided a considerable revenue which was used for continuing the war from bases abroad.

After the subjugation of Norway, 120 officers and airmen and a few battered old aircraft were all that remained of the Norwegian Air Force, by then in England. In 1940 a training centre was set up in Canada at Toronto which became the birthplace of the new modern air force. It was named 'Little Norway' and trained thousands of Norwegians who came from all over the world. This number included many escapees who came across the North Sea to Britain in small boats and others who escaped to Sweden in order to eventually join in the fight.

The Norwegian Naval Air Service operated as part of R.A.F. Coastal Command from British bases while the Army Air Force provided two fighter squadrons. Incidentally, a Norwegian squadron became famous among the Allied air forces' units for its performance and score of victories. In 1944 the two services were amalgamated to form the Royal Norwegian Air Force which was at last an independent arm.

The Norwegians with the R.A.F. wore grey-blue uniforms of British pattern, while those in the Naval Air Service had dark blue naval uniforms. The officers of the former wore a new badge on the peaked cap: this badge was in three separate pieces attached to a shield-shaped grey-blue background. Generals had gold twisted cords as a chin strap, senior officers had two thinner twisted silver cords while the others wore the usual leather chin strap. The old round cap badges, illustrated in the previous plate, continued to be worn on the front of the forage cap while the winged badge, which was at the top of the peaked cap badge, was worn on its own on the left side of the forage cap.

Airmen, as well as officers and N.C.O.s, wore two badges at the front of their forage caps, but without any lace in between. The cockade in national colours was attached at the top and a plain button with the Norwegian Lion below.

The same type of officers' rank insignia was used, but now the stars and the lace were placed at the front of the lapels of the collar of the grey-blue service dress jacket, or on the collar of the grey-blue battledress. The N.C.O.s' ranks were modified to conventional chevrons of silver lace and followed the R.A.F. pattern. The ranks of a Flight Sergeant, wearing three chevrons below the crowned shield of Norway and a Leading Aircraftman at the lower end, wearing a 2-bladed propeller badge, were added.

All wore the 'NORWAY' nationality title on the left upper sleeve and a small Norwegian flag on the right upper sleeve. The nationality title was placed in a frame with trimmed corners; the officers' title was usually embroidered in silver or white thread on grey-blue background while the other ranks' title was in white on dark blue, or black background.

The Pilot's wings remained basically the same although the new wings for Pilots, Observers and Wireless Operators/Air Gunners were now embroidered in silver on grey-blue for those serving in ground based units, and in gold on dark blue for personnel of naval units. Two examples of the former pattern and one of the naval pattern have been illustrated. The Observer's and Wireless Operator/Air Gunner wings were adopted during the course of the war in response to the need for creating new aircrew qualifications.

Netherlands

The interest in aeronautics captured the imagination of many people in Holland as it did in the rest of the world. Early experiments in flight took place some time before the establishment of the Aviation Arm of the Royal Netherlands Army on 1 July 1913. A great deal of enthusiasm, in conjunction with the need to modernise the country's defences before the outbreak of World War 1, lead to a steady development in the field of aviation. The Royal Netherlands Indian Army, in the Far East, raised its own independent Air Service on 20 October 1915 and eventually the Navy also raised its own aviation.

In the period between the wars lack of funds prevented any further expansion and even modernisation of the existing establishment. Therefore the Netherlands possessed only a few, rather obsolete aircraft at the beginning of World War 2. In 1938 the Aviation Arm was renamed Military (i.e. Army) Air Service and hurried preparations for defence were initiated.

The badges of these three different pre-war air branches, and those of new organisations which were raised during the war, have been grouped separately and will be dealt with in different chapters of the text.

Plate 10. Army Air Service–Cap Badges

This establishment was part of the army and therefore field-grey army service uniforms were worn by all ranks; in fact many officers who qualified as pilots or observers were eventually employed as army officers due to the lack of aircraft. Only just before the war, when the Army Air Service was somewhat expanded, were all the aviators employed in their true role, although even in 1940 only about 124 aeroplanes could be mustered.

The service dress and the field uniform were field-grey and the common head-dress for all ranks, with the exception of the generals, was the kepi. The generals wore a peaked cap and a section of the front of the cap band has been illustrated. It shows the cap badge, which was an oval orange cockade in a gold frame, surrounded by a branch of laurel and one of oak leaves with a gold soutache around the top of the cap band and a wavy gold embroidery at the bottom.

The kepi was of Austrian pattern, with a visor covered in field-grey cloth and brown leather chin strap with buckle at the front. The cap band was visible above the chin strap to show the piping on either side and another stripe of piping ran along the top of the kepi. The arm-of-service colour of the Army Air Service was blue.

The national cockade was applied on the upper front of the kepi: the officers' cockade was made of orange silk and gold wire; the N.C.O.s' cockade was all made of silk, while that of the corporals and privates was made of brass with its centre painted orange. A thin cord was attached to the bottom of the cockade and in the loop of this cord there was a button depicting the Lion of Nassau. The cap badge of the lowest ranks had the cord and loop made of metal. Regimental numbers or the Lion of Nassau, made of bronze, were worn on the cap band below the button.

Plate 11. Army Air Service—Rank Badges

Rank distinction was shown in the form of piping on the head-dress while insignia of rank were worn on the collar of the tunic and greatcoat.

The senior officers had three stripes of gold piping on the kepi, one at the top and above and below the cap band; junior officers had gold piping only on either side of the cap band and blue piping at the top of the kepi; warrant officers (W.O.1) had only one gold stripe on the top side of the cap band and N.C.O.s wore only blue piping. The officers and warrant officers had gold piping also on the forage cap while the others had blue piping; the badges or numbers on the forage cap were always painted orange.

All ranks wore field-grey tunics with high collar and blue piping all around it. The generals wore four 6-pointed stars all made of silver, or in gold and silver, and gold embroidery instead of coloured piping. Silver stars and gold bars identified the senior officer while only the former were worn by junior officers. Captains and 1st Lieutenant Adjutants had their first star made of gold and warrant officers (W.O.1) wore a round white metal stud on each side of the collar.

A gold or bronze aircraft engine with propeller, the badge of the air service, was worn on both sides, of the collar.

Stars and bars were worn by officers on either side of the greatcoat's collar while warrant officers in this case wore a special badge: the usual stud but mounted on to brass double bars.

The non-commissioned officers wore inverted-V chevrons, 1·5 cm. in width, on both sleeves just above the cuffs. The sergeants had gold chevrons, the corporals yellow chevrons, mounted on a cloth backing of arm-of-service colour, blue for air force and other corps. The Sergeant 1st Class had a gold soutache above his chevron while the Quartermaster-Sergeant had an extra chevron on the left upper sleeve. The Sergeant-Major Administrator had a gold crown above his chevrons while an Instructor wore a silver crown.

Plate 12. Qualification Badges—Army Air Service

Badges for qualified Pilots and Observers were instituted on 14 October 1919, to be worn on the left breast, above the pocket and eventual service ribbons. The former depicts an eagle in flight above an orange circle, the other shows a winged blue circle and the initial 'W', which stands for 'Waarnemer', i.e. Observer. Up to 1940 these badges were made of gold embroidery but later during the war some metal versions were made in London.

A combined badge for Pilot-Observer was created on 30 December 1930.

R.A.F. wings and half-wings were granted to Dutch aviators who qualified in Britain during the war and which—now known as 'memorial badges'—are still worn by those entitled.

Royal Netherlands Indian Army Air Service

Entirely different qualification badges, made of bronze, were adopted in the colonies for Pilots and Observers on 25 November 1921 and later, on 9 September 1932, a composite badge was made for the Pilot-Observer. The Flight Surgeon's wings appeared in 1940 and all the others, for Air Gunner, Bomb Aimer, Photographer, Wireless Operator and Flight Engineer, were adopted in 1941.

Royal Netherlands Naval Air Service

Qualified flyers of the Naval Air Service wore the badges of Pilot, Observer and Pilot-Observer of the Army Air Service, plus the three special half-wings illustrated. Further details of the insignia of this separate organisation can be found in the chapter relating to Plate 14, where some other naval badges are illustrated.

Trade and Other Badges

Three trade badges were worn until 1940 on the left upper sleeve by mechanics of the Army Air Service. All depict the aircraft engine and with crown and without in gold were worn by Chief Mechanics and Mechanics respectively, while gold or red badges depicting the engine and a 2-bladed propeller were used by Aircraft Mechanics.

The remaining illustrations show nationality titles worn during World War 2 by Dutch airmen in the United Kingdom.

Plate 13. Rank Badges—Army Air Service after 1940

About 250 men, including eight instructors and eighty trainees from the training schools of Flushing and Haamstede arrived in Britain at the end of May 1940, via France. At about the same time, eight aeroplanes of the Naval Air Service crossed the Channel with their crews. They went to form No. 320 (Dutch) Squadron of Coastal Command and were later joined by other Dutch personnel from the East Indies.

Initially Dutch exiles joined the R.A.F.V.R. and from April 1942 volunteers were trained as pilots, and eventually joined No. 320 and other squadrons, mainly Nos. 118 and 167. In June 1943 the latter was re-designated No. 322 (Dutch) Squadron, R.A.F. Men attached to the R.A.F.V.R. wore British grey-blue uniforms and badges with 'NETHER-LAND' shoulder titles embroidered in light blue on grey-blue or dark blue for officers and airmen respectively.

As the Netherlands' armed forces were slowly rebuilt in Britain, during the course of the war a new Dutch air force was organised with its own identity. The Nassau Lion was the main emblem of the new Royal Army of which the Air Service was still part. Only one small section of the army dress regulations published in 1944 was dedicated to the uniforms and badges of the air force, which of course were different to those of the army.

However, the air force badges followed the pattern of those of the parent service, with the exception of the cap badges which were those of the R.A.F.

New 'NEDERLAND' shoulder titles were adopted, in this case with the Dutch spelling, as were badges with the Nassau Lion above the nationality title. The latter were inspired by the army titles which depicted an orange lion and title embroidered on khaki. Some officers of the air force wore for a time the same badge in golden orange embroidery on grey-blue but later the embroidery was changed to light blue, or silver.

Eventually, during the last year of the war, men were recruited in Holland and truly independent national armed forces were established. The Army Air Service and the Netherlands Indian Army Air Service were amalgamated to form the Royal Netherlands Air Force, an independent service. The cap badges were changed to a new Dutch pattern and eventually the nationality title of the arm badge was changed to the motto 'JE MAINTIENDRAI'.

All Dutch aviators in the United Kingdom wore British uniforms and badges with their own nationality shoulder titles. As the war progressed it became apparent that as the former Dutch rank insignia of the officers could not be applied to the new uniforms, new badges had to be devised. Additionally, as the British uniforms had no piping, coloured collar patches were adopted in order to show rank and branch of service at the same time. These appeared in the 1944 dress regulations which became mandatory in February 1945.

Air Force personnel wore Cambridge blue patches, pointed at the top, with rank distinction identified by stars and bars, as worn before the war;

generals' patches had a narrow embroidery at the top which resembled that previously worn by generals on the tunic's collar. Doctors and chaplains wore special breast pocket badges.

The non-commissioned officers wore R.A.F. chevrons and the Leading Aircraftman the propeller badge, but later the original ranks were developed into four sergeants' grades, one Corporal and a Private 1st Class, the latter with one chevron. The 1944 regulations prescribed two Sergeant-Major's badges: the first was a British badge for the service and field uniforms while the second, the Netherlands Royal Crown was worn with dress uniform only. Both badges were worn on the forearm.

Plate 14. Royal Netherlands Naval Air Service

The Royal Netherlands Navy was a very powerful organisation and, as it was partially based in the Dutch East Indies it was not shattered by the surprise attack that hit the Army in Holland.

The Naval Air Service was raised in 1917, with establishments in Holland and in the colonies. In May 1940 all that could be saved of the former was moved to France and later to Britain. In 1942, units of the Naval Air Service in the East moved to Australia and Ceylon following the Japanese invasion of their colonies.

Naval uniforms and insignia were worn by the personnel of this service: it should be noted however that there was not a unique cap badge for all naval officers but corps emblems were placed in its centre, below the crown. The officers of the Air Service had the familiar aircraft engine and 2-bladed propeller, as illustrated.

The personnel of the Naval Air Service was made up of flyers and repairmen, the former with the above-mentioned badge, while the repairmen's badge depicted the silhouette of an aeroplane. These badges were worn on the left upper sleeve by those eligible and were of the same colour as the chevrons, i.e. gold, yellow or red, depending upon rank.

Royal Netherlands Indian Army Air Service

Following the formation of the Army Air Service in Holland, two years later, on 20 October 1915, an aviation branch was also raised in the Dutch Indies, as part of the army.

The uniforms and badges of the new corps were basically the same as those of the army, already described in another volume of this series, and aviators could only be recognised by their arm-of-service colours and by the engine and propeller badge worn on the shoulder straps or on the collar.

A round cockade with orange centre was the head-dress badge in the

East Indies: it was made in gold, yellow silk or cotton, depending upon the rank of its wearer.

Four types of uniforms, the same as in the army, were used before the Japanese invasion. The dark blue, virtually black, ceremonial dress uniform was worn with kepi and an Attila tunic and the former could also be worn with the white uniform in some special circumstances. Below the cockade of the kepi there was the loop and button, as also were shown below the cockades used in Holland, while the round cockade on its own was worn on the cap band of the peaked cap. The Attila had a black collar with blue piping and additional gold lace for generals and senior officers. The arm-of-service badge was worn on the collar.

The badge was worn on the shoulder straps of the white uniform and only the rank was shown on the collar: generals and field officers had the stars on gold lace patches; junior officers, the ensign and warrant officers had their stars or studs attached directly on to the collar. Sergeants had stripes on black patches. The shoulder straps were the same as those of the army, made of gold interlaced cords for generals, woven in gold with a zig-zag pattern for senior officers, plain gold for junior officers and black for N.C.O.s, all with a silver propeller-badge attached.

The two remaining uniforms, the garrison and the field uniform, were both field-grey, with collar patches of different shape on the collar, because their collars were different. Bronze arm-of-service badges were worn on the shoulder straps.

The gold lace patches of the generals and senior officers had coloured piping all around the edges, and in this case junior officers, the ensign and warrant officers, wore black collar patches, the former with a gold stripe inside the edges.

Plate 15. Royal Netherlands Indian Army Air Service—After 1942
The Japanese attack compelled the Dutch units to retreat in 1942 and the Air Service moved to Australia and Ceylon continuing the fight against the invaders. Some pilots were already in Australia before the fall of Java, and due to take over American aircraft. On 1 May 1942 they formed No. 18 (Netherlands East Indies) Squadron, R.A.A.F. This unit was composed of 242 Dutchmen and Indonesians and 206 Australians.

In the same month the Royal Netherlands Military Flying School was created in America, at Jackson, Mississippi, under the command of Major-General L. H. van Oyen. The Royal Netherlands Indian Army and Naval personnel trained there wore American khaki uniforms with Dutch badges; General van Oyen wore his rank insignia on the lapels of the collar of his khaki jacket in the form of four stars above a V-shaped gold stripe, as illustrated.

Trained aviators were sent back to Australia, where in December 1943 they formed No. 120 (Netherland East Indies) Squadron, R.A.A.F., a fighter unit, in Canberra. Later, after the surrender of Japan, No. 121, another fighter squadron and No. 20, a transport squadron, were raised and fought in the Dutch-Indonesian conflict of 1945–50.

The Union of Socialist Soviet Republics

Plate 15. Historical background

Balloons were used in Russia for tactical observation many years before the invention of the aeroplane and an aerostation already existed in the 1890s. Its personnel wore a special breast pocket badge which depicted a winged anchor surmounted by the Czarist double-headed eagle clutching two crossed axes, the whole set on a wreath.

In 1910 six officers were sent to France to be trained to fly aircraft and an Aviation School was formed with branches at Sevastopol and Gatchina (Petersburg).

Some aircraft were bought abroad; later new prototypes were built in Russia and eventually the Imperial Russian Aviation Corps was formed, keeping pace with similar military establishments that were raised all over Europe.

The qualified aviators, i.e. Pilots, were granted a special badge and a similar one, but with an additional telescope was instituted in 1916 for the Observers.

After the Revolution aviation was reorganised under the name of Red Air Fleet of Workers and Peasants which in 1924 was redesignated Soviet Military Aviation Forces.

The personnel of the former wore army uniforms which displayed a light blue arm-of-service colour in various manners according to type of uniform. Uniforms and insignia were standardised in 1919 and in 1922: the latter regulations officially confirmed the use of a metal winged propeller badge for army aviators and a winged anchor for the naval branch.

A special arm badge 100 mm. in width and 63 mm. in height was adopted on 3 April 1920 and a similar one, but with an additional 15 mm. red edge all around, with the inscription 'Exemplary' appeared in September 1922. Some different arm badges were introduced in August 1924 to identify army and naval aviators; their design followed the pattern of the arm-of-service badges of the two branches. A third badge of this type for wearing on the left upper sleeve was issued in 1925 to Aviation Engineers.

In 1924 blue uniforms were adopted; rank insignia previously worn on the forearms was moved on to the collar and collar patches were changed from plain light blue to blue with additional red piping. The arm-of-service badge, to be worn on the collar patch after rank insignia, was also modified; the new one had shorter wings and a rather squarish looking propeller.

The Aviation Engineers, however, kept to army uniforms and had blue collar patches with black piping, ensigned by the winged propeller badge.

New blue uniforms with open collar were adopted in 1935 and saw the Soviet aviators into World War 2.

Plate 16. Head-dress and Rank Badges (1940–43)

The blue uniform was used as parade, service and walking-out dress while for everyday wear khaki uniforms were used, with aviation blue cap bands, piping and patches. In July 1940 an additional grey dress uniform was prescribed for the Marshal of the Soviet Union and for the generals.

A composite badge was worn on the peaked cap while only the red star on blue backing was used on the forage cap.

New collar patches, as well as new uniforms were adopted in 1935: these were light sky blue, with gold piping for officers and black piping for political personnel and other ranks. Oblong patches, 100 mm. × 32.5 mm. in size were worn on the collar of jackets and tunics and larger ones, 110 mm. in height and 90 mm. in width, cut to the shape of the collar were worn on the greatcoat. The winged propeller and rank insignia were placed on the patches as illustrated.

Rank badges in the form of red enamelled diamonds, rectangles, squares and triangles, each corresponding to a class of rank, were introduced in 1924, as a development of pre-existing badges adopted in 1919 and modified in 1922. The structure of ranks was also modified several times during this period as already detailed in another volume of this series.

The senior officers at that time were called senior commanders, the junior officers commanders, and the N.C.O.s were known as junior commanders.

In July 1940 the generals' diamonds were replaced by gold embroidered stars; the illustrations show their patches as worn on the special generals' tunics with stand-and-fall collar. The rank of Marshal of the Soviet Union was above the corps and service cadres and therefore is beyond the scope of this book. The ranks from Colonel to Captain were identified by red rectangles, from four to one.

Gold and red chevrons for wearing by officers on the forearms were adopted in 1935 and modified in 1940. Initially gold chevrons were used by generals and red chevrons by the other officers, but later, in 1940, a single large gold chevron with a narrow red stripe at the bottom, and a gold star above it was prescribed for all the generals except that of the top rank, who had a larger gold star and a red stripe also above the gold chevron. The other officers' chevrons showed a combination of gold and red stripes.

Plate 17. Rank Badges (1940–43)

The lieutenants were identified by square-shaped red enamelled badges, which from three to one were worn on the collar patches; they also wore chevrons on the forearms.

The political personnel were an integral part of the armed forces and were divided into Commissars, i.e. senior ranks, and Politruks, the junior ranks. They wore black instead of gold piping on the collar patches and a red star with hammer and sickle on the sleeves.

A new arm badge for Technical Engineers was introduced in April 1942; a small replica of the same was worn on the collar patches in place of the winged propeller. This one and the arm badges previously mentioned (Plate 15) cannot be classified as 'wings' and flyers on the whole were identified only by the gold wings and star on the peaked cap.

The N.C.O.s wore collar patches with black piping and black central stripe on which the sergeants attached their triangular rank badges. The Sergeant-Major had an additional 3 mm. stripe of gold braid parallel to the piping. Both tunic and greatcoat patches carried a triangular device designed to mark the angle on which the patch was to be set. The tunic's patches had a 5 mm. black stripe in the centre while the stripe of the greatcoat's patches was twice as wide.

Cadets of special schools wore the usual patches with additional embellishments, as illustrated.

Plate 18. Head-dress and Rank Badges (1943)

Uniforms and badges were modified by new regulations which appeared in 1943. New uniforms were adopted with gold shoulder boards 140–160 mm. in length, 65 mm. wide for marshals and generals and 60 mm. for the other officers, with piping and rank insignia.

This plate illustrates the badges of the generals and marshals, the latter's ranks having been created in February of that year. The collar and cuffs of their grey dress tunic were modified in accordance with the regulations issued on 15 January, which prescribed gold oak leaves on the cap band, collar and cuffs of the Marshal of the Soviet Union and gold laurel leaves on the cap band and collar of the generals, and three gold embroidered double bars on each cuff.

On 4 February 1943 a new rank was created, that of Marshal of Aviation, with a silver star 50 mm. in diameter, the same as that of the Marshal of the Soviet Union, on the shoulder boards but with the winged propeller in place of the emblem of the Soviet Union. Later, in October, the marshal's rank was divided into two classes: that of Supreme Marshal and of Marshal and the size of their shoulder boards' star was reduced to 40 mm. to make room for a silver laurel wreath which was added around the star of the former.

The new marshals were authorised collar and cuffs facings in arm-of-service colour, blue in the case of aviation.

New collar patches were applied to the collar of the greatcoat. The buttons of the marshals and generals depicted the emblem of the Soviet Union while those of all the other ranks had the star with crossed hammer and sickle in its centre.

Plate 19. Head-dress and Rank Badges (1943)

The regulations of 15 January 1943 brought many changes to the officers' uniforms also. New tunics had to be adopted on which the new insignia could be applied: all officers had shoulder boards of gold lace for parade and service uniform or made of plain cloth for use on the field uniform. The latter type had blue piping and longitudinal dark red stripes, while the gold shoulder boards had piping and stripes in arm-of-service colour. Senior officers, then still known as commanders, had two stripes and silver stars 20 mm. in diameter while the lieutenants' shoulder boards had one stripe only, and stars 13 mm. in diameter.

The parade dress tunic had collar patches and double bars on the cuffs. The former were blue patches with two or one embroidered stripes according to class of rank which was also shown by the double bars on the cuffs: senior commanders, i.e. senior officers, wore two on each cuff while commanders, i.e. junior officers, had only one.

Aviation personnel had embroidered collar stripes of gold with a narrow silver zig-zag design while Engineering/Technical Staff wore silver stripes with gold zig-zag.

Plate 20. Head-dress and Rank Badges (1943)

The same regulations also dealt with the uniforms and badges of the other ranks: shoulder boards with stripes replaced the collar patches with red triangles and new patches were devised for the collar of the parade/walking-out tunic. The latter were blue, with an additional stripe of gold lace 6 mm. wide, for N.C.O.s, the rank class then known as junior commanders. Engineering/Technical Staff had silver stripes.

Blue shoulder boards with black piping were used on the parade/walking-out tunic: they had additional gold stripes according to rank, metal arm-of-service badge, number and initial of the formation or unit.

The shoulder boards of the field uniform were khaki, edged with blue piping; dark red stripes identified rank.

Cadets had a stripe of gold lace around the edges of their shoulder boards and as they graduated in the same way as the N.C.O.s, they could wear additional stripes as did the latter. Narrower shoulder boards with narrow lace were worn by the cadets of the Aviation Specialists' School. Numbers and Cyrillic letters were worn below the winged propeller as further means of identification.

The 1943 regulations made the blue uniforms obsolete as the Soviet Military Aviation was technically a branch of the Army; aviators wore khaki uniforms with their own arm-of-service colour and badges.

The Naval Aviation existed also as an integral part of the Navy, and its personnel wore naval uniforms but their insignia differed from that of the personnel of the Line. They had army rank titles, wore only shoulder boards and army cuff ornaments instead of naval stripes. The officers of the Aviation Engineering had silver shoulder boards.

Denmark

Plate 20. Miscellanea

Danish military aviation begins in 1911 when the Army Air Service and Navy Air Service were formed, although only one locally built aircraft was available. Two years later four French aircraft were acquired and as a result two Danish officers were sent for training in France.

Denmark remained neutral during World War I and as aircraft were unobtainable from other countries a few seaplanes were built locally; other aircraft were built under licence after the war.

The air services were redesignated Army Flying Corps and Naval Flying Corps in 1922 and four years later a Danish Fokker CV flew from Copenhagen to Tokyo, returning via Siberia and Russia. A reorganisation took place in 1932, planes were bought and built in an effort to reach the planned strength of five Army Flying Corps squadrons, two of fighters and three for reconnaissance, and two naval squadrons.

The German invasion of 1940 cut short this programme: on 9 April German troops crossed the frontiers and aircraft attacked Vaerloese Air Station, north of Copenhagen, destroying a large number of aircraft on the field.

A number of Danish aviators escaped to Britain and to Sweden. Subsequently many served in the R.A.F. and in the Norwegian Air Force raised in Britain, and a Danish dive-bomber squadron was formed in Sweden.

The old flying corps were part of the Army or Navy and their personnel wore the uniforms and badges of the parent service. Only the Pilots were distinguished by the wearing of breast wings.

Danes in Britain wore R.A.F. uniforms with their own nationality titles, embroidered in light blue on grey-blue for officers and light blue on dark blue, or black, for airmen. Twenty-six Danish flyers were killed in action.

France

Flying experiments with balloons and aircraft began in France many years before the official institution of the Military Aviation, in 1910. A Naval branch, called Aviation Service, was formed in the same year.

Great progress was made in a short time and by the outbreak of World War 1 the Military Aviation had twenty-five squadrons, four of which were stationed in the colonies. France was by then the leading nation in the field of aeronautics, a standard achieved by the cooperation of extremely skilled, enthusiastic engineers and aviators of world-wide reputation.

Further, during World War 1, French machines, pilots and specialists were sent all over the world to improve or even to build up from scratch the aviation of various nations. Innumerable problems had to be dealt with to keep up the production of aircraft. Firstly, there was a constant lack of manpower as both the armed forces and industry progressively needed more and more men. New, improved aircraft had to be conceived and built continuously to keep up with the adversaries' technical advance.

The Naval Aviation Service also made its own valiant effort during World War 1 and towards the end of it attempts were made to operate aeroplanes directly from ships, a phase culminating with the launching of the first French aircraft carrier in 1925.

In the years between the wars, French air power declined due to low expenditure programmes and other problems common to many other nations at that time. However, the Military Aviation and the Aviation Service of the Navy were renamed the Army of the Air and Maritime Aviation, respectively, and a programme of reorganisation and modernisation began in the middle 1930s.

By 1935, the metropolitan territories of France were divided into four Air Regions each under the command of a General of Air Division; the 5th Air Region supervised the air force in Algeria. Each region, with the exception of the latter, was formed of two brigades, each in turn composed of demi-brigades, which, commanded by a Colonel, consisted in peacetime of one base and one or two escadres. There were escadres of fighters, of day and night bombers and of reconnaissance aircraft, each divided into two or three groups. These groups, in turn, were formed of two or three escadrilles.

The personnel of the Air Battalions and some independent companies were in charge of administrative tasks.

The Maritime Aviation operated from shore bases along the coastline, which was divided into Maritime Districts as, although another two aircraft carriers went into production they were not finished in time to become operational.

The uniforms of the Army of the Air in use at the beginning of World War 2 were adopted in the years 1934–35. The officers were entitled to wear an evening dress, a full dress and a walking-out uniform, service and field uniform.

French aviators wore dark blue uniforms, the shade of which was known as 'Bleu Louise', although white and khaki uniforms were worn in hot climates.

The evening dress followed the conventional fashion of that time and was worn with peaked cap and cape; it was blue in France and white in the colonies, although a white spencer could be worn in France during summer. Minor variation of detail transformed it into the evening dress for grand, i.e. official and small, i.e. private ceremonies.

The main components of the other uniforms, (the peaked cap, the jacket and the trousers) were basically the same, all made of blue cloth. The blue, white and khaki jackets were single-breasted with open collar and four pockets of the inset or patch type, depending on the type of uniform. Long trousers were usually worn although breeches could be used with the field uniform. The Sam Browne belt, shoes and leather flying jackets were made of black leather, while flying overalls were usually brown.

The warrant officers had uniforms similar to those of the officers with the exception of the evening dress; the sergeants had a walking out uniform, the same as that of the officers and a service dress similar to that of the rank and file. The rank and file wore a blue uniform composed of a peaked cap, jacket with closed, folded collar and trousers, which was used for parades and when walking out; they wore a dark grey uniform when on ordinary duties, composed of a beret, jacket and trousers with puttees.

All personnel of the Maritime Aviation wore naval uniforms and badges and were distinguished by some special aviation badges, which will be mentioned further on in this text.

Plate 21. Army of the Air—Cap Badges

The peaked cap was the common head-dress of French aviators of any rank and was worn with almost every uniform. It was Louise blue with black cap band and black visor and during summer it could be worn with a white cover.

Basically, there were two peaked caps for officers, one for dress uniform and the other for service use. Both displayed insignia of rank and of branch of service. All officers, including the generals, wore gold embroidered wings at the front above the cap band: the wings were the emblem of aviation and above these the generals wore their individual stars of rank, while the other officers wore branch insignia which were usually the formation numbers on their own in the case of metropolitan formations, or above a crescent if the formation was a North African one. A gold anchor was the emblem of the colonial aviation and a star that worn by staff officers. The same badge was worn on dress and service caps. The mechanic and specialist officers had cap badges embroidered on violet velvet and the administrative officers on brown velvet. They also wore coloured collar patches and coloured backing under their rank stripes. These badges, but made of metal, were worn on the tropical helmet.

Gold cords, in lieu of the chin strap, were worn by all officers and warrant officers on the dress cap and by all, with the exception of generals, on the service cap. The service peaked cap of the latter had a conventional chin strap with small gold oak leaves embroidered along its centre. The officers' dress cap carried gold stripes of rank around the cap band, while on the service cap these stripes were embroidered on a padded cloth background, oval in shape, which was fixed on the cap band at the front.

The dress cap band of the generals was ornamented with silver soutache, and two or one rows of gold embroidered oak leaves, depending on rank.

The non-commissioned officer, i.e. from Chief Sergeant to Chief-Corporal, wore a gold chin strap 12 mm. in width and at the top of the cap band a 2 mm. soutache in the same colour, gold or orange, of the chevrons. The blue peaked cap of the rank and file had a blue cap band with orange stripes at the top and bottom. The sergeants wore cap badges as did the officers, while the Chief-Corporal and the rank and file wore the wings on the top and the formation number below, on the cap band, in gold for the former and in orange for the others.

The officers also wore a blue beret with winged star in gold embroidery and small rank insignia. The other ranks had a dark grey beret with rank insignia and metal badges, in gilded brass for N.C.O.s and bronze for the rank and file. A 4-bladed propeller on a wreath was the common emblem, but mechanics wore a winged 2-bladed propeller and other specialists wore different badges.

Qualification Wings

Flying personnel wore wings above the right breast pocket of the jacket; in France these were called speciality insignia and existed in embroidered and metal versions for blue uniforms and linen uniforms respectively. On the evening dress, the wings were replaced by an eagle embroidered in gold.

Aviation personnel had a 5-pointed star between the wings while aerodrome personnel had a cog-wheel instead; formation numbers and badges the same as those on the cap badge were placed in between the wings.

Plate 22. Rank Badges

The officers' rank insignia were worn on the forearms of the blue jacket and greatcoat and on the shoulder straps of the evening dress and summer linen uniforms. As we have already seen, the generals wore their stars on the cap badge as well as on the sleeves.

All other officers wore gold lace stripes, except the Lieutenant-Colonel who had three gold and two silver stripes alternated. Circular stripes were worn above the cuffs of the full dress and walking-out uniform while only short stripes, 35 mm. in length, were used on the other uniforms, stitched on a backing patch, usually blue but in the case of mechanic/specialist or administrative officers violet or brown, respectively.

The evening dress shoulder straps were made of gold lace and bore the rank stripes at the outer ends and the eagle in flight in Louise blue. The Lieutenant-Colonel had three Louise blue and two lighter blue stripes.

The full dress blue jacket had gold shoulder cords while the ordinary jackets had only narrow gold embroidered tabs across the shoulders, near the seam.

Warrant officers and sergeants had shoulder tabs as well, which were a short length of their chevron's lace on blue background. The former wore stripes on the sleeves similar to the officers: the Chief Warrant Officer had a gold strip with a narrow red central line, the Warrant Officer had a silver stripe with red line instead.

All the non-commissioned officers wore 12 mm. chevrons above the cuffs of the blue jacket and stripes of reduced size on the field jacket and on the beret.

The Chief-Sergeant wore three gold chevrons or stripes, the regular, career Sergeant had two chevrons while the Sergeant not in the N.C.O.s' cadre, i.e. conscripted, wore only one gold chevron. The Chief-Corporal and the Corporal wore two orange woollen chevrons, the former with a gold oblique stripe on the left upper sleeve. The Private 1st Class wore only one woollen chevron. Non-flying personnel of aerodrome units wore chevrons instead of short stripes on the field uniform.

Plate 23. Collar Patches

The flying officers did not use collar patches while non-flying officers wore collar patches instead of the qualification wings of the former. The mechanics and specialists wore violet patches and the administrators wore brown velvet patches with their formation number in gold in the centre.

These patches were sewn on the corners of the lapels of the collar and therefore have been illustrated in different shapes. The ground officers' patches were smaller as they carried the formation number only, while the other ranks' patches had piping, numbers and often badges as well and were necessarily larger. In addition, the rank and file wore a tunic with closed, folded collar, which was wider than the lapel of the N.C.O.s.

All the other ranks of the flying and ground cadre wore collar patches made of Louise blue felt, with coloured piping consisting of stripes of Russia braid, numbers and badges, that identified the branch of service and unit of the wearer. Flying personnel wore also metal qualification badges on the breast.

The branch colours of the piping were as follows:

Colours	Branch of Service
Green	Fighter Interceptors
Yellow	Mixed Formations (escadre)
Scarlet	Bombers
Sky blue	Intelligence, Reconnaissance and Observation
Violet	Aerodrome Personnel
Ash grey	Air Battalions and Companies
White	Metereology
Orange	Balloon Battalions

Personnel of units grouped into a corps wore three stripes of piping instead of two.

The numbers and badges on N.C.O.s' collar patches were embroidered in gold, while the rank and file had orange formation numbers and badges. Some specialisations were identified by means of badges shown on the collar patches: a winged 5-pointed star was worn by qualified pilots and observers; a winged wheel was the badge of qualified aerostate personnel, observers of captive balloons, pilots and mechanics of airships. A winged grenade was worn by air gunners, wireless operators and flight engineers and a cog-wheel by ground specialists.

Personnel of North African formations wore a crescent and those of the colonial aviation had an anchor, without formation number.

Personnel in possession of a certificate of aptitude to be engaged as aircraft mechanics wore a half cog-wheel above a thin chevron on the left upper sleeve, in gold or orange depending on rank. Stevedores wore an interlaced stripe of braid.

Plate 24. Qualification Badges—Army of the Air

These badges were made of metal and were worn on the right breast of the tunic by other ranks with flying qualifications.

The badges, which included a 5-pointed star, were intended for aircraft personnel while those with the steering wheel were worn by airship and balloon personnel. The winged 2-bladed propeller was worn by aircrews, i.e. flight engineer, bomb aimer, wireless operator, air gunner, etc., serving with aircraft and airships alike. Cadet pilots wore all-silver badges.

Maritime Aviation

The Maritime Aviation was a branch of the French Navy and therefore naval uniforms and basic badges were worn by all ranks.

A special arm badge distinguished the aviators: it was worn on the left sleeve and depicted, regardless of rank, a gold embroidered winged anchor with a star in the centre. Some pilots, but not officers, eligible for the special title of Superior Pilot or Chief of section had a golden 5-pointed star and a wing on each side of the collar.

Metal badges were worn on the right breast, regardless of rank, by qualified personnel. They were rather similar to those of the Army of the Air, although a cable substituted the wreath and an anchor was appropriately added on the background. Wings, as usual, stood for aviation, the 5-pointed star represented aircraft flying qualifications while the steering wheel identified airship or balloon qualifications.

Free French Air Force

After the German invasion of France many French aviators joined the R.A.F., but the majority of them were eventually drawn into French units. The status of the Free French in Britain was somehow different from that of other exiles as they could exert more pressure on the British Government because they already had fighting formations in Africa and the Middle East.

Although the Free French Armed Forces depended on the Allies for equipment, they never entirely adopted foreign uniforms and kept to their own badges.

The Cross of Lorraine, the French emblem dating back to the time of the Crusades, became the symbol of the Free French in 1940, and some new badges were made showing this cross. It appeared on the new air force officers' cap badge and in the centre of the new helmet badge. A breast badge of the Free French Air Force was also introduced and two different variations were used: one made in London had the French tricolour starting with the red at the top while the colours of a badge made in Syria started with the blue, on the left.

The Free French Naval Force was also organised with British and American help and, with it, a small Naval Aviation unit which took part in the landing in Sicily and later in the South of France. These aviators wore qualification badges, made in London, which were the same as the previous ones except for an additional Cross of Lorraine.

The first formation of the Free French Air Force raised in Britain was the No. 2 Fighter Group 'Île-de-France' or No. 340 (French) Squadron, R.A.F., formed at the end of 1941 by personnel of the ex-Army of the Air and Maritime Aviation.

The No. 1 Fighter Group was raised at Rayak, in Syria, in September 1941; this was the 'Alsace' unit formed by the Strasbourg and Mulhouse escadrilles, i.e. flights. Later this group was transferred to Britain where it was number No. 341 Squadron.

It should be noted that at this time the French used to name their air groups after French Regions and the two flights of the group after towns of that region. Previously the air formations were identified by numbers only.

Another group which eventually, in 1943, became No. 342 (French) Squadron, R.A.F., a bomber formation, originating from units in the French African colonies, fought in Abyssinia and North Africa where it was known as the Free French Squadron. Later it was named Lorraine Group, formed by the Metz and Nancy Flights.

Another bomber formation that fought in North Africa was the Bretagne Group, with the Rennes and Nantes Flights. It originated from units in the Tchad and, after the North African campaign the Bretagne Group was based in Sardinia and later in France.

Breast pocket badges were worn by the personnel of groups and of some escadrilles and specimens of these have been illustrated. These badges were made of metal and enamel and depicted the coat of arms of the French regions and towns the formations were named after. Often several variations of the same badge can be encountered as they were made at different times, by different manufacturers, in different countries.

Plate 25. Free French Air Force

The Military Air Lines were organised in 1941 as a necessary means of communication and way of supplying the Free French units dotted around all over the world. Its badge symbolised this deployment exactly.

The No. 3 Fighter Group Normandy was formed in Syria in 1942 and initially was formed by three flights, Le Hâvre, Rouen and Cherbourg.

Later, for a period, a fourth unit named Caen was part of the group. The Normandy was sent to the Soviet Union in November 1942 where it remained until the end of the war. During this time it was awarded the battle honour Niémen and therefore it became known as the Normandy-Niémen Group. Nationality shoulder titles were worn on the blue walking-out uniform: the French version was worn on the left and the Russian version on the right upper sleeve. A shoulder title 'Normandy', written in cyrillic characters, was used as well. Various enamel badges were adopted each showing the common motif of the two leopards of Normandy.

Another two groups, the Artois and the Picardie, were formed in Africa and in the Middle East for coastal defence duties. Later the Nos. 329 and 345 (French) Squadrons, R.A.F., were based in Britain and eventually were transferred to the Continent where they took part in the final stages of the war.

By 1944, the Free French were back at home where they were able to reorganise their forces and to strengthen them with new manpower. The Free French Air Force was renamed once again the Army of the Air and some badges were modified appropriately as the new recruits were not, obviously, Free French.

French, American and British uniforms were used, depending on the source of supply. The former was worn as a walking-out uniform and on formal military occasions when available, but the other two types of uniform were more common at that time.

Rank badges were also worn in different positions and a new rank, that of Sergeant-Major, was introduced also. Long stripes and chevrons were still worn on the forearms of the Louise blue French uniforms or short ones, 5 cm. in length, on a blue background, were worn on the forearms of the khaki American jacket, or on the shoulder straps of the American blouse. Rank insignia were on the shoulder straps of the British uniform and all summer shirts.

The Cross of Lorraine was eliminated from the officers' cap badges which were embroidered on branch of service colour as in the following list:

Colours	Branch of Service
Black	Flying Cadre
Violet (velvet)	Mechanics' Cadre
Brown (velvet)	Administrative Cadre
Bordeaux red (velvet)	Medical Personnel
Blue	Air Police

The Army of the Air was formed by the following corps, the personnel of which wore one or the other colour of the above list:

Officers	Other Ranks
Flying Cadre	
Air Officers Corps	Flying Personnel Corps
Sedentary Cadre	
Air Mechanic Officer Corps	Mechanical Personnel Corps
Corps of the Officers of Air	General Service Personnel Corps
Administrative Services	
Air Commissariat Officers Corps	
Air Police Officers Corps	Air Police Personnel Corps
Military Air Engineers Officers Corps	

These were followed by the officers and other ranks of the Air Medical Service, Chaplains, Musicians and female personnel.

In order to further define the individual's duties, the pre-war qualification badges were reinstated, with the exception of the airship qualifications that had become obsolete. Also breast wings, embroidered on Louise blue backing, were reintroduced officially and others, for Equipment and Aircraft Mechanics, were worn on the sleeve.

Belgium

Plate 26. Officers' Cap and Qualification Badges

The Belgian Military Aviation was created in 1910 to test and fly balloons and aircraft. At that time the Aviators' Company was in charge of aircraft, becoming the Aviation Militaire in 1915. It expanded considerably during World War 1, in line with the air forces of the Entente and later, in the early 1930s, the Belgians adopted the training methods of the R.A.F. as by then many British machines were in use.

By 1940 the Military Aviation's primary role was that of army support although aviation and anti-aircraft were technically part of the Territorial Air Defence.

Flying personnel wore grey-blue uniforms while ground personnel wore khaki uniforms, the same as the army's. The latter wore distinctive collar patches, sky blue with scarlet piping. The grey-blue uniform was similar to that of the R.A.F., with long trousers or breeches and riding boots. All officers had a black cap band with the Aviation's badge at the front, sided in the case of generals by a vertical gold bar on each side. The senior officers had gold piping at the top of the cap band. All wore the tricoloured Belgian cockade just above, in the centre, at the front of the peaked cap.

A similar but larger winged badge was worn on the left sleeve and later during the war on the left breast above the ribbons. This badge, embroidered in gold for officers and in silver for other ranks on dark blue or black background, depicted the crowned Royal Cypher of the reigning monarch, sided by wings. Flying personnel other than pilots wore the same cypher but with one wing only. Aerostate officers who were qualified balloon observers wore a gold embroidered balloon on the sleeve of the jacket.

The non-commissioned and other ranks of the ground personnel wore a special badge, a propeller on a disc, on the left side of the forage cap and on both shoulder straps, in the latter's case above the regimental number (1, 2 or 3). A similar badge with additional initials 'EP' standing for École de Pilotage, i.e. Pilots' School, existed.

The rank titles and corresponding badges were the same as those of the Army; as the officers and warrant officers of the flying cadre wore no collar patches their stars and bars were embroidered directly on the collar. The 3-star badge was often worn with the single star above as well as below the two stars.

As a result of the German Blitzkrieg in 1940 the majority of Belgian aircraft were destroyed on the ground and eventually many aviators joined the R.A.F. and were grouped to fight in Nos. 349 and 350 (Belgian) Squadrons, R.A.F., both fighter units, which eventually combined a score of 161 victories. During this period they wore British uniforms, R.A.F. rank insignia and were distinguished by nationality titles only.

Plate 27. Formations' Badges

Initially these badges were painted on the aircraft but later metal and enamel versions were adopted for wearing on the left pocket of the jacket. The three aviation regiments of 1940 were divided into groups which in turn were divided into escadrilles, squadrons. The abbreviated numbers that identify the badges start with the squadron number and end with the regimental number. The Roman numbers identify the group.

The 1st Aviation Regiment had the role of Army Corps observation, the 2nd was a fighter regiment while the 3rd Regiment's role was reconnaissance and bombing in support of the ground armies.

The Pilots' School badge depicted a penguin because of the hesitant behaviour of this non-flying bird—an association with the school's young cadets.

Yugoslavia

Plate 27. Cap and Qualification Badges

The Royal Yugoslav Air Force traced its origins to the Military Aviation of the Kingdom of Serbia. On 24 April 1912 six Serbian officers were sent to France to train as pilots and the nucleus of an air force was formed during the same year with its first headquarters near the town of Nish. During the ensuing Serbo-Bulgarian War, on 8 March 1913, the pilot Miodrag Tomich dropped four ordinary cannon grenades on a bridge on the River Bojana; this action is recorded as the first bombing mission ever made.

After World War I Yugoslavia became an independent nation and Serbs, Croats and men from other ethnic groups joined the armed forces. Some had served already as aviators in the Austro-Hungarian Air Force during the war and therefore were recruited in the newly formed Military Aviation, which was initially a branch of the Army. Designers and technicians, many of whom had had practical experience abroad set up an aeronautic industry that as well as producing aircraft on licence, built and tested its own.

The German-Italian attack on 6 April 1941 caught the Air Force with an array of different aircraft and the disproportion of the forces in the field left no doubt of the final outcome.

At that time only the officers and sergeants wore grey-blue air force uniforms while the other ranks still wore the field grey uniforms of the Royal Yugoslav Army.

The officers had a special badge embroidered in gold and silver on the peaked cap; the generals had two rows of gold laurel leaves on the visor and the senior officers one row only. A similar but smaller badge was worn by officers and was attached at the front of the forage cap. The N.C.O.s, corporals and privates wore the oval cockade of army pattern.

Pilots and observers wore special metal badges above the right breast pocket of the jacket.

Plate 28. Rank Badges

The officers wore rank badges on the sleeves and shoulder boards similar to those of army officers, but on sky blue backing. The generals had gold twisted shoulder cords; the officers wore gold shoulder boards which in the case of junior officers had a central blue stripe. Silver pips identified rank in the usual manner.

On the sleeves the generals wore gold 6-pointed stars above an eagle in flight while the other officers had stripes below the eagle. The eagle was worn by flying personnel only. The four junior officers wore gold stripes 5 mm. in width while the senior officers had the same stripes but worn above a larger one, 15 mm. in width. Stripes and eagles were placed above a black background.

The Sergeant-Majors wore shoulder boards similar in shape to those of the officers but made of sky blue cloth; all had four gold pips, and three, two or one stripe, depending on the class of rank. The 1st Sergeant, Sergeant and Corporal wore shoulder straps, the former with blue piping.

Many Yugoslav airmen managed to escape to the Middle East and to Britain where eventually they manned two R.A.F. squadrons. At that time the Yugoslav government was reorganised in Britain and eventually new regulations were published in order to standardise the Yugoslav badges, by then worn on British uniforms.

The air force officers obtained new shoulder straps, made of grey-blue cloth on which the junior officers wore from one to four gold 6-pointed stars, the senior officers wore the stars, from one to three, below a crown and the generals had crossed swords between the crown and the stars. The Field-Marshal (Voivoda) wore the crowned White Eagle of Yugoslavia on the shoulder straps and a gold crown above the cuffs. Stripes, as before, were worn on the cuffs, but the generals wore from one to three large gold stripes below a 6-pointed gold crown. The officers of the Anti-Aircraft wore grey-blue uniforms with the usual pre-war air force cap badge on the peaked cap but also wore black facing on the collar, gold stripes on the shoulder straps and crossed cannons ensigned by the eagle in flight above the cuffs. Rows of gold leaves were embroidered on the peaked cap's visor as before the war.

Later, when Communist orientated Yugoslav forces were organised under the name of National Liberation Army, new rank badges were adopted for wearing on the sleeves. They consisted of a combination of 6-pointed stars and stripes, made of silver for N.C.O.s and gold for officers.

The United States of America

Plate 29. Historical Background

As early as the American Civil War balloons were used for tactical observation by the Union and Confederate armies and in 1892 a Balloon Section was attached to the telegraph branch of the Signal Corps. Balloons fitted with telegraph apparatus were used again during the Spanish-American War and in 1902 a balloon unit was formed at Fort Myer, Va.

On 1 August 1907 an Aeronautical Division was created in the Office of the Chief Signal Officer 'to study the flying machine and the possibility of adapting it to military purposes'. The new organisation was composed of one officer and two enlisted men.

The first successful flight took place at Fort Myer in 1909 in a Wright brothers' biplane piloted by Orville Wright, with Lieutenant (later Major General) Frank P. Lahm as a passenger; it lasted 1 hour, 20 minutes and 40 seconds. Lieutenants Lahm and F. E. Humphreys subsequently became the first qualified pilots.

On 18 July 1914 an Act of Congress created the Aviation Section of the Signal Corps and in the following September the 1st Aero Squadron was formed at San Diego, California, with a strength of sixteen officers and seventy-seven enlisted men.

The first badge of Military Aviator, which was instituted on 27 May 1913 depicts the American Eagle clutching the crossed flags of the Signal Corps, the whole suspended from a tablet; it is a reminder of the early association of the aviation with the corps. The badge was made of 14 kt. gold and was intended as an award compared to the marksmanship and gunnery badges, not as a qualification badge.

The aviators wore, of course, the collar badges of the Signal Corps, but by 1917 manufacturers added small wings to the original badges of the Signal Corps. These unofficial officers' badges became very popular with the result that many variations appeared on the market. In most cases the wings were made of silver and were attached to the centre of the bronze badges (A, B); small and larger variations of this pattern were in existence. Another variation of the aviators' collar badge shows the wings in bronze at the top of the badge, which has no torch (C). Officialdom had eventually to recognise the need for a special badge for aviators and on 27 April, 1918 a new collar badge was authorised showing the usual signal device with a winged hemisphere superimposed on its centre (D). A variation of this badge shows a smaller hemisphere and somewhat straighter wings. The enlisted men wore the same device but on a bronze disc.

When World War 1 broke out in 1914 the American military aviation had five aircraft while by the end of that war it had received no less than 2,500: these figures reflect the expansion of the Aviation Section, which in May 1918 was renamed the Air Service Branch of the Signal Corps. Later in 1926 it became the Air Corps and in 1941 Air Forces. Aviation broke its links with the Signal Corps in August 1915 and was under the General Staff until March 1942, when it became autonomous (U.S. Army Air Forces) as was the case with the Army Ground Forces and Army Service Forces.

The United States of America entered the first conflict on 6 April 1917 and sent an Army Expeditionary Force to Europe. Earlier many American volunteers had joined the Allied cause, for instance Major Raoul Lufbery, French by birth, who at the age of six in 1891 emigrated with his parents to the United States. Later he became the mechanic of a famous French stunt flyer. During the war he joined the Escadrille Lafayette, composed of American volunteers and in April 1918 became the commander of the U.S. 94th Aero Squadron. He was killed on 19 May 1918. Captain Eddie Rickenbacker, the American ace with 25 victories, became the squadron commander the following September. The 94th Aero Squadron's badge, painted on its planes, depicted a top hat, painted with stars and stripes, which flies through a ring.

The first qualification badges were authorised on 15 August 1917. The American Shield sided by wings was granted to the Military Aviator (1) and the shield with one wing only to the Junior Military Aviator (9). However, this ruling was changed on 27 October when a star was added to the wings of the Military Aviator (8) and the original badge, without star, was given to the Junior and Reserve Military Aviator.

The original badges were embroidered in silver wire, with gold initials 'US' on the shield, on dark blue cloth background. As each badge was individually hand embroidered many varied in style and shape (1, 3); by the summer of 1918 manufacturers had introduced metal badges, in three separate pieces mounted on a dark blue felt background (2, 4). Subsequently the three parts were attached together (6, 10) and finally the blue background was discarded and a pin was fixed at the back of the badge (7).

In the meantime, as has been already mentioned, in October 1917 the Junior and Reserve Military Aviator changed from the half-wing to the full-wing without star, and the half-wing became the badge of the Observer until 29 December 1918, when the letter 'O' with one wing was adopted as his badge (11) and the previous one was definitively discarded. Eventually metal 'O' badges appeared (12), then badges with the rounded 'O' were introduced (13) until finally, on 21 December 1918 a solid metal pattern was adopted (14).

On 29 December 1917 wings embroidered in white silk were authorised for Military Aeronaut and Junior and Reserve Military Aeronaut, with and without star respectively. Such badges were also made in silver embroidery and later in metal also.

The Enlisted Pilot's wing and the large square sleeve patch illustrated at the bottom of this plate were also made of white silk and, as usual, variations exist of both: the latter is a 1918 specimen; early badges had numbers at the top to identify the squadron; enlisted airmen wore only the propeller below the number, mechanics wore a ring around the propeller and balloon mechanics had a balloon in place of the propeller.

An official badge depicting a bomb sided by wings was worn during the first war by Bombing Military Aviators.

A process of standardisation started after the end of World War 1: on 25 January 1919 the definitive qualification wings made of oxidised silver were introduced for Military Aviator and Junior and Reserve Military Aviator (see Plate 36, Pilot); for Military Aeronaut and Junior and Reserve Military Aeronaut (see Plate 36, Balloon Pilot); for Observer Qualified as Pilot and a half-wing was awarded for Observer.

On 12 November 1920 more changes took place: the winged American Shield became the badge of the Airplane Pilot and another badge, an airship superimposed on wings was created for the Airship Pilot, the Observer's half-wing was abolished and a round winged 'O' with blank centre was adopted for the Airplane Observer and the winged balloon (see Plate 36, Balloon Pilot) became the badge of the Balloon Observer. More changes took place later, as will be explained in connection with the wings illustrated on plate 36.

In 1926 embroidered badges were re-introduced for wearing on the wool service coat.

Plate 30. Cap Badges and Other Insignia

Various cap and collar devices worn by American aviators during World War 2 are illustrated in this plate. Although the U.S. Army Air Forces was the organisation that eventually became the modern U.S.A.F., the U.S. Navy, Marine Corps and Coast Guard had their own aviations also. The personnel of these organisations wore the normal cap badges of their parent services, i.e. the U.S. Army, Navy, etc. but in the context of this book these technically become air force insignia.

All ranks of the U.S.A.A.F. wore appropriate cap badges as their counterparts of the U.S. Army. Aviation cadets wore the winged propeller instead. Towards the end of World War 1 the N.C.O.s of the Air Service used a bronze unofficial cap badge which depicted the winged propeller surrounded by a wreath similar to that of Warrant/Flight Officer illustrated.

The winged propeller was the branch of service badge of aviation and as such was worn by all ranks on the collar. The first development of this badge has been seen already in the historical background of this chapter. The actual winged propeller device was adopted on 17 July 1918, on its own for officers and on a disc for enlisted men. These badges were made of blackened bronze although the propeller was usually silvered. Many slightly different variations exist because these badges were manufactured in America, Britain and France. A smaller badge was worn by officers on the shirt's collar.

After that war gilded badges were introduced for officers and brass ones for enlisted men; the officers' propeller was still made of silver. Olive-drab plastic badges were used by enlisted men during World War 2. The branch of service badge was worn together with the 'U.S.' national insignia and during the last war the officers wore these badges in pairs on the service jacket, the 'U.S.' on the collar, the winged propeller on the lapels. The latter and the rank badge were worn on the shirt's collar. Enlisted men wore the 'U.S.' disc on the right and the branch badge on a disc on the left side of the collar. The arm-of-service colours of the Air Corps were ultramarine and orange.

The aviation personnel of the U.S. Navy, Marine Corps and Coast Guard wore the cap badges of their parent services although naval aviation officers and aviation cadets of the U.S.M.C. had different badges attached on the left side of the garrison cap. The Naval Aviator and Naval Aviation Observer wore a miniature gold metal aviation insignia on the left side of the green winter working garrison cap until the spring of 1943 when they were obliged to follow naval regulations, and replaced it with a small replica of the usual cap device. Aviation Cadets of the U.S.M.C. wore a bronze winged propeller on the garrison cap and shoulder straps during the same period and a gold and silver device with the dress uniform. Eventually they became part of the U.S. Navy until commissioned and the above-mentioned badges were abolished.

All the officers and the Chief Warrant Officer of the U.S. Navy Aviation wore the normal naval cap badge made of metal or embroidery, the eagle of which faced left until May 1941, and right as its correct placing should be, from then on. The American Shield, below the eagle reappears on the cap badges of the U.S. Coast Guard of which it is the major insignia, and on its own is worn on the shoulder boards, above the cuff stripes. It is worn in white or blue version according to uniform, on the cuffs of enlisted men.

All ranks of the U.S. Marine Corps wore the Marine Corps emblem on the head-dress and collar. The larger badges were worn on the peaked cap in gilt and silver for officers' dress uniform, brass for enlisted men's dress uniform and bronze for all ranks' service uniform. The rope of the officers' badges was free of the anchor while in the case of enlisted men the rope and the anchor were in one piece. There was no rope in the smaller badges worn on the garrison cap, and on the collar. In the latter case badges were worn in pairs.

Plate 31. Officers' and Warrant Officers' Rank Insignia

The aviation personnel used the rank insignia of their parent service, i.e. the U.S.A.A.F. had those of the U.S. Army, the U.S. Navy Aviation those of the U.S. Navy and so on, in accordance with dress regulations.

The metal badges illustrated in the centre of this plate were common to all. These rank badges were primarily used by the U.S. Army and U.S. Marine Corps while the main rank insignia of the U.S. Navy and Coast Guard were worn in the form of stripes on the sleeves and on the shoulder boards. Their rank titles also differed from those of the first two services.

The rank of Flight Officer was instituted in the summer of 1942 as an opportunity for cadets who did not qualify for a commission in the U.S.A.A.F. The rank was equivalent to that of Warrant Officer, Junior Grade.

The marines' warrant titles and badges differed from those of their army counterparts: initially, during World War 2, the Chief (commissioned) Warrant Officer wore a gold and blue bar and had the title of Chief Marine Gunner, Chief Pay Clerk, Chief Quartermaster Clerk or Chief Quartermaster Clerk (A. and I.). The latter initials were added to distinguish this title of the Adjutant and Inspector's Department from that of the Quartermaster's Department. The Warrant Officers (not 'chief') wore their departmental insignia in lieu of a rank badge.

Later the titles were changed to Commissioned Warrant Officer and Warrant Officer, and different rank badges were adopted also.

The main uniforms of the U.S.M.C. were the blue dress, the green service uniform and light khaki shirt and trousers for summer wear; on the latter smaller rank badges were used, about five-eighths of the normal size for shoulder straps. Gold/Silver or bronze departmental badges were used according to uniform.

There were blue, green, grey, white and light khaki naval uniforms, with rank insignia on the sleeves, on the shoulder boards or on the collar accordingly. Both the sleeve stripes and shoulder boards were worn on the overcoat only, otherwise only one or the other type of insignia was used.

The flag officers wore stars and the fouled anchor on their shoulder boards or stripes on the cuffs, contrary to the other officers who had stripes only, on both.

There were stripes of 2 in. in width for the flag officers, $\frac{1}{2}$ in. and $\frac{1}{4}$ in.

for the other officers in gold and black variations, the latter for naval grey working uniform and the green working uniform of aviation officers.

The Chief (commissioned) Warrant Officer and the Warrant Officer were identified by broken stripes of different width as illustrated: gold and blue or black and grey, according to uniform. (See also Plate 34.) Small metal rank badges were worn by the officers on the light khaki summer shirt.

Plate 32. Army Aviation N.C.O.s' Rank Badges

The Non-commissioned Officers of the U.S.A.A.F. wore army pattern chevrons, consisting of actual chevrons and arcs, on both upper sleeves. Technicians' grades were introduced in January 1942 and they wore the initial 'T' below their chevrons. Some unauthorised versions were manufactured and worn by Line N.C.O.s before and during World War 2, with a small winged propeller in place of the Technicians' 'T'.

All chevrons were 80 mm. in width and were machine embroidered in khaki (O.D.) silk or woven in sandy grey silk (for summer shirt) on a dark blue background.

Oblique single khaki (O.D.) stripes on the left forearm identified each three years of honourable Federal service. Small yellow inverted chevrons on the left forearm each identified six months of World War 1 overseas service while yellow stripes were granted for World War 2 service. One yellow inverted chevron was worn on the right forearm for each wound received in combat before the introduction of the Purple Heart.

Plate 32/33. Army Aviation Cadets' Rank Badges

The Flying Cadets originally wore slate blue uniforms with black chevrons similar to those worn by the cadets of the U.S. Military Academy. Later they were re-designated Aviation Cadets and were given khaki uniforms with khaki chevrons on dark blue background. The chevrons worn on coats are 80 mm. in width while those worn on overcoats are 190 mm. wide and, as shown on Plate 33, they differed considerably from the former.

Plate 34. Petty Officers' Ratings—U.S. Navy and Coast Guard

Besides the more obvious similarity in dress between the U.S. Navy and the Coast Guard, the latter in peace-time depends from the Secretary of Treasury while in war-time it comes under the control of the Secretary of the Navy.

Both had the same rating badges, which consisted of the eagle, the arc and chevrons and speciality mark that in the case of ordinary petty officers were blue on white background for white uniform, while for the blue uniform the eagle and speciality mark were white and the chevrons red, all on blue background.

The Chief Petty Officer wore officers' type uniforms, the arc above the chevrons and, on the blue coat, had the option of wearing silver or white eagle and speciality mark. The Chief Petty Officer of outstanding record, i.e. with not less than 12 years of service, three consecutive good conduct awards, or equivalent qualifications, wore gold chevrons with silver embroidered eagle and speciality mark.

Personnel of the Seaman Branch (Boatswain's Mate, Quartermaster, Fire Controlman, etc.) wore the rating badge on the right upper sleeve while the personnel of Aviation and other branches had the badge on the left sleeve. Initially the eagle always faced left as did the eagle of the officers' cap badge but during World War 2 some new regulations ordered that the eagle of the rating badges should always face towards the front of the wearer, regardless if placed on one or the other sleeve.

Only speciality marks were shown on rating badges, never distinguishing marks (Plate 37) which were proficiency badges.

Enlistment stripes of the same colour as the chevrons were worn one for every four years of service on the forearm, below the rating badge. White cuff markings were worn on blue and white dress jumpers and identify Fireman or Seaman class. They were 120 mm. long, made of a narrow white ribbon, 5 mm. in width, sewn on both cuffs.

The aviation cadets did not wear the line star on the cuffs and shoulder boards until 1943 and the winged propeller worn by U.S.M.C. cadets was abolished at about the same time.

The personnel of all branches of the U.S. Coast Guard wore their distinctive shield above the stripes both on the cuffs and shoulder boards or in the case of ratings and seamen on the right forearm. The shield was about 25 mm. in height and was embroidered in gold for officers and warrant officers; in silver for chief petty officers and white or blue for enlisted men, according to uniform. The shield was black on green winter aviation uniform.

Plate 35. N.C.O.s Rank Badges—U.S. Marine Corps

The U.S. marines used three types of chevrons: gold on red background for the dress blue uniform, green on red for green winter uniform and on light khaki for summer shirt.

The N.C.O.s of the Line have chevrons joined by arcs while those of the Staff had theirs joined by ties, i.e. straight bars. The marine advanced into the Line or Staff careers by becoming a Private 1st Class (6th Grade) but only when he reached the 3rd Grade rank did the arc or the tie identify the branch to which he belonged. Aviation N.C.O.s wore ties under their chevrons as aviation was one of the seven specialisations of Staff.

The lozenge within the First Sergeant badge was adopted during World War 2 while the badge with three chevrons and three arcs was worn by the Sergeant Major and Master Gunnery Sergeant (1st Grade Line). The Master Technical, Paymaster and Quartermaster Sergeant wore the 1st Grade Staff badge. Two arcs were used by the Gunnery Sergeant and two ties by the Technical and Supply Sergeants and Drum Major, one arc by the Platoon Sergeant and one tie by the Staff Sergeant. The remaining ranks were those of Sergeant, Corporal and P.F.C.

Before September 1942 the rank badges were worn on both upper sleeves but new orders were issued on the 9th of that month, which prescribed the use of chevrons only on the left sleeve.

Enlistment, or service stripes, were worn one for each four years of service.

Civil Air Patrol

The Civil Air Patrol was a civilian volunteer organisation which became an auxiliary body of the U.S.A.A.F. by Executive Order of 29 April 1943.

The C.A.P.'s activities included patrolling the coastal water in an anti-submarine defence role, air courier and transport services, etc., as well as its pre-military training programme for youths between 15 and 18 years of age.

The organisation derived from the Office of Civilian Defence from which it adopted the basic blue disc and white triangle badge. A C.A.P. aviation wing existed in every State and its members wore military uniforms and ranks with the badges illustrated on this plate. All except cadets had red shoulder straps as further means of identification.

The officers wore army type rank badges and the N.C.O.s had chevrons but on red background. Qualification badges were worn by those entitled above the left breast pocket and one short gold stripe was worn on the left forearm for each period of six months service. Small blue, red and white triangles of cloth were worn above the left pocket in lieu of merit awards.

The Duck Club badge was worn by personnel who had made a forced landing at sea. Some shoulder sleeve insignia of C.A.P. have been illustrated in Plate 39.

Plate 36. Qualification Badges

The wings worn during World War 2 were made of sterling silver, as embroidered badges were finally abolished by the regulations issued on 16

March 1938. The appearance of the actual wings was standardised to a design by Herbert Adams, adopted in 1919.

On 10 November 1941, three classes of Pilot's wings were authorised thus distinguishing pilots with longer service and a higher average of flying hours.

The winged balloon was reinstated to the Balloon Pilot and a new badge was authorised for Balloon Observer, with an additional 'O' on the balloon. Balloon pilots with 10 years of service, who had piloted military airships or motorised balloons for 100 hours were granted a new badge with star and the qualification of Senior Balloon Pilot. A new badge was adopted on the same date for the Technical Observer.

More badges appeared in the following year: that of Navigator has an armillary in its centre and that of Bombardier depicts an aerial bomb on a target. The qualified Service, Liaison and Glider Pilot were granted new badges with the initials 'S', 'L' and 'G' in the central shield. The Liaison Pilot wings were worn regardless of rank by men assigned to organic air observation of the field artillery. Later the granting of this badge to enlisted men was discontinued.

The Aircrew Member wings were worn by men regularly assigned aircraft personnel who had shown proficiency in performing their duties. The centrepiece of the Aerial Gunner wings shows appropriately a flying bullet; was adopted on 29 April 1943 for qualified gunners if regular members of a combat aircrew.

The Flight Surgeon wings originally adopted were gold-plated and were changed to silver in September 1944. Smaller gold wings, 5 cm. in span, were adopted in 1943 for the Flight Nurse and subsequently were changed to silver.

The Flying Instructor badge was authorised in metal, in January 1919 and re-issued in March 1943 to be worn, now embroidered in gold colour, on the right sleeve at 10 cm. from the end.

The wings of the Women's Air Force Service Pilots (WASPS) illustrated belonged to the 319th Training Detachment and the 'W1' identified first class graduation. WASPS were engaged in non-combat flying missions and training duties under U.S.A.A.F. control. Earlier during the war women were engaged in ferrying aircraft under the organisation known as Women's Auxiliary Ferrying Squadron (WAFS), but later women were deployed in other fields of duty as well. Another pattern of women's badge depicts a plain diamond between the wings.

Wings were adopted by the U.S. Navy only at the beginning of 1919 although official approval to the project was stated in Change 12 to Uniform Regulations, issued on September 1917. A gold metal badge with a pin at the back was finally chosen as the Naval Aviator's device. The badge did not change a great deal although the original pattern was solid, and later versions varied in style more than in design.

A Naval Observer's badge appeared in 1922: it consisted of a gold embroidered fouled anchor with the rope forming the shape of an 'O' in the centre, sided by one single wing. Five years later a similar badge, but made of gold metal and with the American Shield in place of the 'O' was authorised to identify the Balloon Observer. The aircraft Observer's badge used during World War 2 depicted an anchor within an 'O' in silver finish, sided by gold metal wings. The badges of Flight Surgeon and Combat Aircrewman were adopted during the course of the war.

The U.S. Marine Corps and Coast Guard used the same qualification badges as the U.S. Navy. Some smaller wings, approximately half size of the normal ones were worn by officers on the evening dress and the white mess jacket.

Plate 37. Naval Speciality and Distinguishing Marks

The speciality marks identified the specialisation or trade of a seaman and the badge eventually became part of his rating insignia, and was worn above the chevrons. The distinguishing marks were only proficiency badges and were worn usually on the sleeve if regulations did not prescribe otherwise. Dark blue badges were worn on white uniform and vice versa.

Air Carrier Contract Personnel—A.T.C., U.S.A.A.F.

The personnel of this organisation wore army uniforms with special bronze badges and one, two or three stripes on the sleeves of the service jacket, or short bars on the shoulder straps of the trench coat.

The National Memorial at Kitty Hawk, N.C., in remembrance of the first flight performed there by the Wright brothers in 1903 is the badge of the Air Transport Command (Plate 39) and is in the shape of a small round disc worn on the shoulder straps and by non-supervisory ground personnel on the service and garrison cap as well. A large version of the same badge was worn as a shoulder patch on the left sleeve with a number in a circle embroidered below.

Personnel sent on overseas duties wore the non-combatant patch on the right sleeve: it depicts the letters 'US' in black on a white equilateral triangle (side 9 cm.) on a black square background.

Plate 38. U.S. Army Air Forces Shoulder Sleeve Insignia

From 1921 to 1942 the fuselage marking of American aircraft depicted a white 5-pointed star with a round red centre set on a round blue background; the red disc was abolished in August 1942 and two white bars, one on each side of the emblem, were added in June 1943. Until the following September the emblem was outlined in orange, and later in blue. The star with red centre remained however the main emblem in all war-time insignia, except for the earlier patch of the U.S.A.A.F. authorised on 20 July 1937 for wear by personnel of GHQ Air Force. The badge symbolised a spinning propeller and was executed in the colours of the Air Corps, ultramarine blue and orange.

The U.S. Army Air Forces was created on 20 June 1941, following a decision to convert the existing Air Districts (Northeast, Northwest, Southeast and Southwest) into Air Forces, numbered from 1st to 4th respectively. The first two districts became Air Forces on 9 April, the SE Air District on 24 May and the SW Air District became the 4th Air Force on 31 March 1941.

A new shoulder patch was approved for personnel of the U.S.A.A.F. on 21 March 1942, and later for the continental Air Forces as well.

On 5 February 1942 the Far East Air Force was redesignated the 5th Air Force, the Caribbean Air Force the 6th, the Hawaiian Air Force the 7th and the Alaskan Air Force became the 11th Air Force. The reorganisation of the former, heavily engaged against the Japanese, was completed by the following September in Australia; its patch was authorised on 25 March 1943. The 6th Air Force was formed to protect the Canal Zone and the Caribbean area while the 7th and the 11th became engaged in active operations in the Pacific. The latter with headquarters in the Aleutians covered the northern Pacific theatre of operations. The badge of the 7th was approved on 21 May and that of the 11th on 13th August 1943.

The 8th Air Force was activated at Savannah, GA., on 28 January 1942 and by the following May some of its units were transferred to Britain from where, on 27 January 1943, it carried out its first bombing raid over Germany. The 8th's patch was officially approved on 20 May.

In the meantime, on 12 February 1942, the 10th Air Force was activated at Patterson Field, Ohio, and became operational in the India-Burma area, where soon afterwards it began ferrying supplies to China, across the Himalayas. This task developed into the setting up of the China Air Task Force which on 10 March 1943 gave birth to the 14th Air Force at Kunming, China. The latter's badge, approved on 6 August 1943, depicted a flying tiger in memory of the American Volunteer Group (The Flying Tigers) in China which had been taken over by the 23rd Fighter Group, 10th Air Force, in July 1942.

The U.S. Army Middle East Air Force was formed in the summer of 1942 in Egypt and on 12 November it was redesignated the 9th Air

Force, a tactical formation which was transferred to Britain in 1944. Its badge was approved on 16 September 1943. The 12th Air Force was raised at Bolling Field, D.C. in August 1942; during the following November it supported the invasion of North Africa and as a tactical formation it took part in the invasion of Italy. Another formation, the 15th Air Force, was activated on 1 November 1943 in the Mediterranean area for strategic operations. The 13th Air Force was raised already in January in the Southwest Pacific area.

After the raising of the 15th Air Force and the transfer of the 9th to Britain, the U.S.A.A.F. and R.A.F. achieved a perfect balance of strategic and tactical power and were able to co-ordinate strategic raids on central Europe from the west with the 8th and from the south with the 15th Air Force, thus the U.S. Strategic Air Force was formed as a supervisory headquarters. The 20th Air Force, with headquarters in Washington, D.C., directed the strategic air offensive against Japan. The Mediterranean Allied Air Force was a combined U.S. and British organisation.

Specialists' Cuff Insignia

The five triangular badges illustrated were authorised on 25 January 1943 to be worn by specialists of the U.S.A.A.F. on the right forearm 10 cm. above the end of the sleeve of all uniforms, except fatigue, on which the badge is worn on the left breast pocket.

The last two badges with the winged propeller were worn on the sleeve by cadets.

Plate 39. U.S. Marine Corps, Civil Air Patrol, etc. Shoulder Sleeve and Cuff Insignia

Cloth badges were very seldom granted to the marines and in March 1943 only, the commandant of the Corps authorised the wearing of a limited number of shoulder sleeve insignia by personnel of the first three marine divisions and of some other formations. The shield-shaped Aircraft Wing patches were adopted at that time but were later replaced by the kite-shaped patches with a winged Corps' emblem in the centre.

Personnel of the 1st Amphibious Corps were granted large blue patches with white stars symbolising the Southern Cross and different badges in the centre, on a red background. The Aviation Engineer's badge depicted a winged castle.

The Air Transport Command was formed from the conversion of the Ferrying Command on 20 June 1942 and was composed of a Ferrying and an Air Transportation Division. The original Air Transport Command was redesignated Troop Carrier Command. There were two patches of

Air Transport Command, one on light blue and the other on yellow background, the latter for ferrying formations.

The High School Victory Corps, as well as the C.A.P., ran programmes of training for youths and 'Air' was only one of the H.S.V.C.'s specialisations. Others were entitled Land, Sea, Community and Production, each represented by a badge. The basic badge of this organisation was a thick red 'V', for Victory, on which round specialisation badges were superimposed at the top.

During World War 2, the personnel of the Civil Air Patrol (see Plate 35) wore three main shoulder patches and rectangular patches on the left sleeve above the cuff. The latter identified personnel of Active Duty units or one's speciality. The Active Duty Units performed various tasks: the Forest Patrol, for instance, was basically concerned with fire prevention while the Coastal Patrol was engaged in coastal security duties and the Southern Liaison Patrol kept watch on the Rio Grande.

Most of these badges were worn until 1947 when a reorganisation took place; later blue patches with white emblem were worn on the forearm.

Italy

Plate 40. Historical Background

Captain of Artillery Carlo Piazza made the first operational flight in Libya on 25 October 1911, during the Italo-Turkish War. He flew on another thirty operations during that campaign and a colleague of his recorded a total of fifty-four operational flights.

A new era had begun, with its accompanying new weapons of destruction. On 24 May 1915, when Italy entered World War 1, only a few dozen planes were available whereas at the end of that war (4 November 1918) 1,758 Italian aircraft dominated the sky, and 1,784 aviators had fallen in the meantime. Among the many that should be remembered, I mention only Major Francesco Baracca, who scored thirty-four victories until finally, in June 1918, he was shot down by rifle fire.

The aviators wore the grey-green field uniforms of the Army and the badges of the branch of service to which they belonged originally, usually the Artillery and Engineers. Aircraft personnel had a small propeller added to the centre of their cap badges, while personnel manning airships and balloons wore their own special devices on the cap badges. Qualification badges were worn on both sleeves, halfway between the shoulder and the elbow: the qualified pilots had an eagle surmounted by the Royal Crown and observers wore a winged sceptre and an 'O'. When the observer took on the additional task of a machine-gunner the 'O' was replaced by an 'M'. The balloon observers had a small dragon instead of the sceptre.

Cloth titles were also worn at the outer ends of the shoulder straps by the men of some units. Antonio Segni, a future president of the Republic of Italy, served as an aviator of the artillery and wore a self-explanatory shoulder title.

The 87th Squadron was named 'La Serenissima' after the city of Venice and bore the large, handsome Lion of St. Mark painted on its planes. Supreme Headquarters employed this squadron on many missions of long range reconnaissance, including the flight on Vienna, inspired by the poet Gabriele D'Annunzio, himself an observer. This expedition was mounted on 9 August 1918 with the purpose of dropping leaflets on the Austrian capital and was accomplished by seven planes which flew a distance of over 1,000 kilometres in one hour and fifty minutes.

After the flight, the squadron's command was taken over by Captain Natale Palli, one of its participants, whose brother, a pilot in another squadron, was shot down on 3 November, a day before the end of the war.

Later, on 20 March 1919, Natale's plane crashed on the Alps while attempting the Padua-Paris raid.

The first shoulder title of the squadron read 'SQ' above 'SERENIS-SIMA' in white on black, but in 1919 its late commander's name was added on to the shoulder titles.

A new pilot's badge was adopted at about that time: it depicted a winged propeller. For Mechanics the propeller was replaced with an aircraft engine. Army uniforms were still in use but with an additional cobalt blue collar; qualification wings were moved on to the breast in the early 1920s.

In 1923 the 'Regia Aeronautica' became a service in its own right and new blue-grey uniforms were adopted for its personnel. Peaked caps and forage caps appeared when army personnel were to continue to wear the old soft kepi for another ten years. The new officers' jacket had an open collar, patch pockets with flaps and a cloth belt. Trousers or breeches were worn in different circumstances. Warrant officers, sergeants, and officer cadets had similar uniforms, with single-breasted jackets and gilded buttons while the rank and file wore tunics with high closed collar until 1934 when new jackets were introduced. Both patterns were single-breasted, initially with wooden buttons covered by a fly patch and later, from 1932, with five exposed brass buttons. Both had four patch pockets with flaps and shoulder straps. Grey-blue breeches and puttees and black boots completed the uniform.

The officers' grey-blue uniform is still more or less the same in the 1970s. White and khaki uniforms were used during summer and in hot climates, and greatcoats of usual style were used in winter. The rank and file's clothes were greyer, lighter in colour than those of the higher ranks, because they were made of a rather coarse melton cloth, while the latter had their peaked caps, jackets and trousers of gaberdine cloth of a considerably darker shade.

The newly formed Royal Aviation instituted qualification badges made of metal, to be worn by all entitled on the left breast, above the ribbons. The pilots wore a crowned eagle in flight, while the other aviators had wings, with a central device. The Commander, 2nd Officer and Crew of airships, still popular at that time, had crowned crossed anchors as the wings' central device, with red enamel in the crown of the former, a plain gilt badge for the 2nd Officer and the same but with silver crown for the Crew Officer. Balloon observers and aircraft observers of the army had their own wings which appear in the 1931 dress regulations, although probably they were adopted much earlier.

The same regulations show that the engineers in charge of balloons still had their own cap badge in 1931, with a small balloon embroidered in the centre of the engineers' badge. A larger balloon, embroidered on grey-green, was worn on the upper left sleeve.

Army personnel who, as aviation pilots, had taken part in the Italo-Turkish War 1911–12, or World War 1, or subsequent operations in Albania from November 1918 to August 1920, or any military operation in Libya or Somaliland from October 1912 to 1923, could apply to the War Ministry for the concession of a special silver badge: a winged sword with crown superimposed. Civil airline pilots who had flown over 1,000,000 km. were granted a special badge in the late 1930s.

From 1923 to the early 1930s all flying ranks had double wings and the Royal Crown on the shoulder straps, while specialists wore brass winged badges instead.

Plate 41. Cap Insignia

The spread eagle surrounded by a laurel wreath and surmounted by the Royal Crown was adopted in 1923 as the badge of the Air Force. Large gold embroidered badges were worn on the peaked cap by officers, warrant officers, and sergeants, and smaller gold badges on the forage cap; the airmen usually wore the forage cap and therefore had only small cap badges, machine- or hand-embroidered in yellow thread.

The generals, from the rank of General of Air Squad and above, and Inspector General of the Aviation Engineers, wore cap badges with purple-red backing under the crown, while all the other officers, except Chaplains, had blue backing. The Chaplains had violet backing under the cap badge's crown, and a red cross on the chest of the eagle.

The laurel branches of the flying personnel's badges were plainly joined at the bottom while specialists had an additional roundel, with a badge or device, in its centre. These latter cap badges were abolished during the course of World War 2. Another distinguishing feature was the coloured piping and backing to rank insignia.

By the 1930s the Royal Aviation was a very complex but functional organisation, and besides the Flying Role, the following specialisations existed also:

Specialisation		Badge
Services Role		Savoy Knot
Aviation Engineers {	Engineers' Role	Roman helmet
	Technical Assistants' Role	Roman helmet above crossed hammer and axe
Commissariat Corps {	Commissariat Role	Oak wreath
	Administrative Role	Laurel wreath
Medical Corps		Aesculapius staff

Specialists' Role—divided into categories, each with its appropriate badge. (See Plate 45.)

Some officers of Flying Role had also badges with the roundel with the number of the Stormo, or higher formation they belonged to.

The whole of Italy was divided into Territorial Air Zones (4) plus the air forces in the colonies: nine planes formed a Squadriglia, two or more Squadriglie formed a Gruppo, two or more Gruppi a Stormo. During the war two Stormi were joined under the Air Brigade and Air Divisions and Air Squads were organised as well, as part of an Air Army. The general organisation of the Royal Aviation however was modified from time to time to take losses and dispersion of strength into consideration, as expeditionary forces were deployed on all battle fronts, including the North of France, for the Battle of Britain (Italian Air Corps).

Officers' and warrant officers' rank was shown by stripes on the cap band, with an additional gold embroidered greca in the case of the generals. These insignia corresponded with the rank badges worn on the sleeves of the service uniform, except for warrant officers who all wore only one single stripe on the cap band, regardless of class of rank. Contrary to the stripes on the sleeves, which were individually stitched on a cloth backing, the cap band stripes were woven in one piece with 2 mm. grey-blue or coloured space between one stripe and the other. They were slightly narrower than those of the sleeves. The sergeants wore a plain cap band, without any rank distinction on the head-dress.

Plate 42. Officers' Rank Badges—Service Uniform

The conventional shoulder straps of the officers' service uniform were replaced in the early 1930s by small shoulder tabs, which identified the class of rank and the branch of service of the wearer. The tabs for the jacket were 55 × 28 mm. while those for the greatcoat were 65 × 30 mm. in size, and were applied on the shoulder at 4 cm. from the sleeve's joint.

The generals had gold lace tabs, the senior officer had two gold embroidered edges of 1.5 mm. each on uniform's cloth, and the junior officer had one gold edge only. Branch of service badges were embroidered in the centre of the shoulder tabs. Black tabs with violet piping, gold edgings denoting class of rank and a gold embroidered square cross were worn by Chaplains. They also had a large red cross stitched above the left breast pocket of the service uniform.

All the officers of the Flying Role, including the generals, wore a sceptre on their shoulder tabs while the others wore their appropriate badges, already described, and coloured piping around the tabs, as below:

Specialisation	Colour
Services' Role	Emerald green
Aviation Engineers { Engineers' Role	Crimson
Technical Assistants	Black
Commissariat Corps { Commissariat Role	Red
Administrative Role	Black
Medical Corps	Methilene blue
Specialists' Role	Black

The same colours, in the form of a cloth backing, were shown under the rank stripes, on the sleeves. Initially, in the 1920s, the officers of the services had sleeves' stripes without the square loop. Branch of service colours were abolished in the first years of the war.

As the officers' service jacket had no cuffs the rank stripes were applied at 90 mm. from the lowest edge of the sleeve and were 80 mm. long; smaller, gold embroidered stripes were worn on the sleeves of the ceremonial uniform. The generals' greca, stripes and loop were always embroidered in gold wire, on felt matching the uniform's colour or coloured background for the commanders of branches other than the Flying Role. They were known by different rank titles, such as Major- or Lieutenant-General, or Inspector General in the case of the Aviation Engineers, due to the fact that they did not command an operational formation.

The General of Air Squad had two stripes as did the general of Division but with a crown below the greca and usually commanded a Territorial Air Zone, in army terms corresponding to an Army Corps. The General of Air Squad 'in Command' of an Air Army wore the crown and an additional sceptre below the greca.

The crown superimposed on crossed swords identified a Promotion for War Merit and, as in the Army and the Navy, were as follows:

In silver on uniform's colour backing for holders of junior officers' rank at the moment of promotion.

In gold on uniform's colour backing for holders of senior officers' rank at the moment of promotion.

In gold on red backing for holders of general's rank at the moment of promotion.

The officers' rank stripes were made of gold lace: the narrow ones were 12 mm. in width and the larger base stripes for senior officers were 22 m. in width.

The same type of badges, but without the loop, were worn by all officers including generals, on the front, left side, of the forage cap.

Plate 43. Officers' Shoulder Boards for Full Dress Uniform
The full dress uniform for officers of the Royal Aviation was abolished during the first years of the war: it consisted of the usual grey-blue peaked cap, jacket and trousers, but with a white shirt and black tie, with additional shoulder boards, dress waist belt, blue sash, sword, metal decorations and medals. Aiguillettes were worn by eligible personnel. The wearing of the blue sash, sword, decorations and medals only was permitted after 1941. The sword, steel helmet and a brown leather Sam Browne belt with pistol and breeches were worn on parades and similar military events.

The generals' shoulder boards were made of grey-blue gaberdine material or coloured velvet or cloth depending on the branch of service, covered with gold lace at the top, with grey silk at the bottom, leaving the arm-of-service colour to protrude all around the sides. The other officers' shoulder boards, except those of the Chaplains, were made of uniform's cloth, like the generals', with, in some cases, an additional underlay of coloured velvet or cloth forming a piping all around. Chaplains had black shoulder boards with violet, often purple, piping.

Twisted gold cords were added on those of the generals and senior officers, while junior officers had twisted gold cords with blue specks woven into it. The Royal Crown, the branch of service badge and the rank badge were embroidered in the centre, between the cords.

The shoulder boards of the Evening Dress Uniforms for winter were similar but their background was black instead of grey-blue.

The warrant officers' and sergeants' full dress uniforms were similar to that of the officers, although the latter were not entitled to wear a sword, and their waist belt was made of brown leather; neither wore the blue sash. Their full dress shoulder boards were also different from the officers' ones: they were made of blue woven silk, with gold stripes for warrant officers, without rank identification for sergeants. All bore the branch of service badge, in gold embroidery or metal at the outer ends. It should be noted that warrant officers and sergeants of Flying Role had a wing as their badge, and not the sceptre of the officers.

The airmen's full dress uniform had brass buttons and the Air Force badge, in brass, on the shoulder straps.

Officers' Shoulder Boards for Colonial and Other Uniforms
Another type of shoulder boards was worn on khaki and white colonial uniforms and on the summer ceremonial uniform: they were similar to the previous pattern but, in the case of generals and senior officers, with a gold embroidered stripe instead of the gold twisted cords. Junior officers had plain boards, with the Royal Crown, branch and rank insignia.

153

The background to the cap badge and shoulder boards of the colonial uniforms was grey-blue; no rank insignia were worn on the sleeves.

Warrant Officers' and N.C.O.s' Rank Badges
The service uniform of warrant officers and sergeants had grey-blue shoulder tabs 55 × 28 mm. in size, with branch of service badge and, those of the warrant officers, with rank stripes at the front. The sergeants wore gold chevrons and the airmen red chevrons on both upper sleeves.

Plate 44. Qualification Badges
During the last war qualification badges were worn by pilots, observers and air crew members. The first two were modified in the early 1930s to suit the fashion of that time. The realistic design of the previous badges were replaced by a stylish, contemporary conception and the fascio was added at the bottom.

Earlier, some pilots were granted special badges with coloured letters enamelled in the centre. Pilots who had flown high velocity planes had a red 'V' on the badge, others had an 'S' for flying at high altitude and those who crossed the Atlantic were granted the badge with a blue 'A'. These daring exploits of early aviation were recaptured in the new 'Fascist' badges. Some unofficial wings existed as well: the pilots of the 'Green Mice' Squadron had three small green enamelled mice on their wings.

However, although pilots took to wearing their new badge with the fascio, the vast majority of observers wore the new pattern badge without the fascio.

All air crew members, regardless of specialisation wore a circular badge, 18 mm. in diameter, ensigned by the Royal Crown. At least three versions of this badge existed: one was made all in white metal, another had red enamel inside the crown and another had also blue enamel in its centre. Later the crew members bought privately and wore on uniform some unofficial wings which were their arm-of-service badges, illustrated in the next plate, with added wings. Two types of these wings were made, in white metal with realistically drawn wings and in grey metal with streamlined wings.

Aviators were granted metal breast badges for good performance in their deployment: there were three grades of badges, in gold, silver and bronze, although in the case of the former only the central device was gilded. During the war the badges of the first two grades appear to have been made in aluminium, and the central device of those of the first grade were painted yellow.

A special badge for the Parachute Battalion of the Air Force was adopted in 1942, and was worn until the end of the war.

The Parachute Battalion of the Air Force was raised in the spring of 1942 as a special task force to be deployed in the projected assault on Malta; i.e. its companies should have occupied and restored the island's airfields so that they could be used immediately by the Axis air forces. Later this project was abandoned and on the 16 November the Battalion arrived at Bizerta by sea and was subsequently employed as an infantry unit, which was swallowed up in the North African battlefield.

All ranks wore Army-type parachute uniforms, berets, collarless Saharian jacket and baggy trousers, all made in grey-blue cloth. Air Force cap badges and shoulder tabs were worn together with parachutist's collar patches and arm badge. Air Force rank stripes were worn on the cuffs and stars, as with the Army, on the left side of the beret.

A special badge, the pilot's eagle with parachute, was adopted in 1942 as the qualification insignia of the Parachute Battalion of the Air Force. The same badge was re-introduced after 1943 for the newly formed parachute units of the Republican Air Force.

Plate 45. Arm-of-Service (Category) Badges

While the Air Force officers were divided into Corps and Roles the airmen were divided into categories, depending on the specialisation, identified by small round badges on the shoulder straps. Technical Assistants of any rank wore the same badge and others of these badges were also worn by the officers of the Specialists' Role, while in the case of Administrative personnel, the officers' badge was a laurel wreath, the airmens' a capital 'G', which stands for Governo.

All these badges are self-explanatory; for instance the badge of Photographers depicts the camera's shutters, the Armourers had a grenade above crossed rifles, etc. The 'M' in the Fitter's badge stands for Montatore and the additional 'S' stands for Strumentista.

Arm Badges and Miscellanea

Assault Pilots, Bandmasters and Fencing Instructors wore special badges, embroidered in metal wire, on the upper left sleeve halfway between the shoulder and the elbow.

A peculiar wide brimmed straw hat used to be worn by airmen when in fatigue uniform in hot climates, and the tally illustrated was worn on this hat. The only other badges on this uniform were the national five-pointed stars, woven in white on a circular grey-blue background.

Other badges also existed: the Air Force in the Aegean had a beautiful enamelled breast badge 38 × 30 mm. in size, surmounted by the crown, and groups and squadrons had also their own badges. The badge of the 1st

Squadron depicted Disney's Donald Duck, rolling up his sleeves and the badge of the 4th Bomber Squadron depicted Pluto and a bee. The badge of the 1st Interceptors Group, illustrated, shows the Rampant Horse which, during World War 1 used to be the emblem of Captain Baracca's squadron.

These badges were the small replicas of the formation emblems worn on flying overalls, one of which, of the Red Devils, is illustrated on the cover of this book. After September 1943 this became the badge of the 5th Squadron of the 2nd Interceptors Group and from 1957 to 1959 it became the National Acrobatic Patrol, of the 6th Air Brigade.

The Air Force of the Italian Social Republic

After the Armistice of 8 September 1943 with the Allies, by then well on their way to occupy all the south of Italy, the new Republican Air Force was formed in the north, while the Regia Aeronautica continued its existence in the south. The latter did not change badges and therefore this text will now only deal with the Air Force in the north.

During this period the Aeronautica Repubblicana raised three groups of fighter-interceptors, each with three squadrons, which were numbered from 1st to 9th, and minor units most of which were eventually absorbed in the groups; the Autonomous Group of Torpedo Aircraft, with three squadrons, plus a complementary, HQ Training Squadron. There were also two transport groups, each with three squadrons, and a liaison unit. At this time the anti-aircraft artillery was placed under the command of the Air Force. All the necessary support units, training schools and administrative echelons existed as well making this small Air Force into a fully independent and very effective service.

Towards the end of 1944 Germany retrieved its operational formation from its Southern flank, the defence of which was then left to the Republican Aviation, already mauled by the Allies' air superiority and frustrated by constant lack of fuel.

Although new regulations were published which introduced new uniforms and new badges the vast majority of aviators continued to wear the old uniforms and the old badges, from which the Royal Crown was simply cut off. A new cap badge was machine-woven for the airmen as the crown could not be eliminated from the old badge without defacing it altogether.

A new national insignia replaced the stars on the collar: it was known as the 'gladio' and depicted a Roman sword with 'Italia' inscribed on the hilt, superimposed on a wreath of oak. As with the previous stars, the generals wore gold badges while the other ranks had white metal ones.

Two special badges were worn by personnel of the Torpedo Aircraft Group: the first illustrated on the left was made of metal and was worn on the right breast pocket while the larger badge on the right was embroidered in gold and was worn on flying jackets. In June 1944 ten aircraft of this group attacked the harbour of Gibraltar and later operated in the Adriatic and Aegean seas. In less than one year 223 men of the group, including thirty pilots, lost their lives. Statistics based on the production and losses of aircraft during the course of World War 2 indicate that an Italian pilot had only an average 4 hours of operational flight before being shot down.

China

Plate 46. Cap and Other Badges

Experiments in the field of aviation started before the foundation of the Republic of China in 1911, as in the second year of the reign of Emperor Hsuan Tsuan in the Ching Dynasty the General Staff established an airplane experimental factory at Wu-li-tien, east of Nanyuan.

Later some regional air forces were formed and finally in 1920 Generalissimo Chiang Kai-shek activated the Aviation Bureau at Ta-sha-tou, Canton. This organisation was composed of a headquarters with the Adjutant and General Affairs Divisions, and the 1st and 2nd Airplane Groups.

General unrest prevented the Central Government from asserting its control over the whole of China and other regional air forces remained active at the time. In 1934 an American Mission provided some more aircraft and later, after the Japanese attack of 1937, the Soviet Union also aided the Chinese government. The first confrontation recorded between Chinese and Japanese aircraft took place over the Chien bridge, Hangchou, on 14 August 1937, in which six Japanese planes were downed. During the long struggle that followed the Chinese Air Force lost air supremacy and eventually an American Volunteer Corps, known as the Flying Tigers, was raised in the spring of 1941, with a strength of about ninety Curtiss P-40B fighters.

These planes were made famous by the genial shark's face painted at the front. Initially the A.V.C. defended the Burma road to China, was later moved to China and eventually was absorbed into the 10th U.S. Air Force.

During World War 2 Chinese aviators wore khaki uniforms, the same as those of the Army, but with different badges. The Officers' and N.C.O.s' badge for peaked cap consisted of the national emblem above gold or silver wings respectively, while the other ranks wore the national emblem only, at the front of their soft cap.

Rank insignia were initially worn on the forearms and were embroidered in gold wire, as separate stripes but in 1940 they were moved on to the shoulder straps. Metal bars had appeared by then and eventually new badges were introduced with the bars joined together by two strips of metal.

The winged propeller was worn on both sides of the tunic's collar: several variations of this badge existed during the war.

The Chinese armed forces made use of a great number of fully written identification badges; one of triangular shape has been illustrated. Below the national emblem the wording means 'Aeronautic Committee', the second row of characters means 'AAA School', the third reads 'Corporal (Rank) Chang Te-kung (Name) and the last reads' Issued in 1942'.

Some other badges with Chinese lettering, and a set of collar badges of the General Staff Academy, have been illustrated.

Bulgaria

Plate 47. Cap, Collar and Rank Badges

The Bulgarian armed forces were comprised of an aviation branch during the Balkan War of 1912–13 and subsequently during World War 1. However, in both instances the branch was disbanded after the wars, as foreign machines flown by foreign pilots were used; further, as Bulgaria took the side of the Central Powers, it was forbidden to possess an air force after World War 1.

The Bulgarian Air Force was raised in 1937, once again as a branch of the Army, and although grey-blue uniforms were adopted for the new service they were worn mainly by officers and senior N.C.O.s. The grey-blue and the army khaki uniform had the same pattern, only the colour of the material changed.

The peaked cap had a short leather visor, with cords for officers and senior N.C.O.s and leather chin strap for the other ranks. Tunics with stand-and-fall collar were later replaced by jackets with open collar, although the former was always worn by the lower ranks, to the end of the war. The officers and N.C.O.s had breeches, or occasionally long trousers, while the other ranks had trousers tucked in high boots.

There were embroidered and metal versions of the winged cap badge of the aviators; the generals wore gold badges, the others silver badges, as silver and sky blue were the distinctive colours of the Air Force. Gold, as a rank distinction, was worn by the generals on the shoulder boards and collar patches also.

The tunic's collar patches of generals and officers have been illustrated, the other ranks had plain oblong sky blue or sky blue patches with silver stripes according to rank. Corporals and privates had a button at the rear end of their tunic's patches, but no button on the greatcoat's collar patches. The officers wore oblong patches with button on the collar of the greatcoat.

The officers wore silver shoulder boards on tunics and greatcoats: these had sky blue piping and central stripes, two for the senior officers and one for the junior officers with silver stars for all ranks. The King's monogram or other badges often appeared on shoulder boards and on other ranks' shoulder straps.

Plate 48. N.C.O.s' Rank Badges

Senior N.C.O.s had a stripe of silver lace around the loose sides of the shoulder straps, and narrower stripes to denote rank. The Corporal wore only one narrow stripe.

The rank of Potential Officer, practically a warrant officer's, was instituted during the war as the highest N.C.O.s' rank.

Germany

Historical Background

At the beginning of the century the Germans saw the potential of flight only as a means of aerial reconnaissance and employed airships for this purpose. The first aircraft were constructed in 1910 and soon after the Military Aviation Service and the Naval Air Service became operational, and were equipped with both airships and aircraft.

During World War 1, although the interest of most nations converged on to aircraft, Germany continued developing the airship which had a wider operational range than the former. Aerial freedom was Germany's only counterpart to the sea blockade that surrounded her, and long range bombing raids were the direct result. Airships and large bombers were deployed on these raids and the former became obsolete only after the invention of the incendiary bullet, which the Germans could not match by the invention of a non-combustible gas to fill their airships.

The organised fighter-interceptor warfare developed only after the invention of a synchronised gear which enabled a machine-gun to fire through the propeller. The inventor was A. Fokker, a Dutchman working in Germany. The purpose of aviation, which started as aerial reconnaissance had developed into a new kind of warfare, aimed at obliterating the enemy's machines from the air.

Aviators like Oswald Boelcke, Baron Manfred von Richthofen and many others accumulated scores of victories until eventually most of them were in turn shot down.

The Military Aviation Service was organised by the Corps of Engineers in 1913 and thus engineer uniforms were worn by all ranks, although the officers seconded to the Air Corps during World War 1 continued wearing the uniform of the corps they belonged to originally. On the pre-war uniform all wore a winged propeller badge on the shoulder straps, the other ranks with the unit's number below, but the use of the latter was discontinued early in the war.

The first qualification badges, worn on the breast, were adopted in January 1913 for Army and Navy Pilots and one year later a badge was granted to the Observers. The Aviator Commemorative Badge was adopted at the same time. The Naval Pilots operating on land and Naval Observers received badges in May 1915 and smaller, commemorative badges for Naval Pilots and Observers were granted in October 1916. The Air Gunner badge was adopted in January 1918. Bavarians wore similar badges but with the Bavarian crown instead of the Imperial crown at the top. There were Bavarian badges for Pilots', Observers', Air Gunners' and Aviators' Commemorative Badges. The bronze badges for Airship Crews were adopted in August 1920.

After World War I, the clauses of the Treaty of Versailles prevented the raising of a conventional air force and flying was an activity confined to the sports clubs formed by a few enthusiasts. In March 1933 these clubs were amalgamated in a single institution, the Deutscher Luftsport-Verband which had branches specialising in aeroplane, glider and balloon flying. The members of this association wore uniform and insignia, which disguised also the officers of the air corps, the organisation of which was secretly set up at about the same time.

The German Air-sport Association was embodied in the National Socialist Flying Corps in March 1935: the latter was a politically orientated para-military organisation that technically prepared its members for active service in the Luftwaffe. The corps' rank insignia and titles were modelled on those of the S.S.

The Luftwaffe, the German Air Force, came into existence on 1 March 1935 and expanded rapidly in the following years: the anti-aircraft was part of it thus unifying the air defence branch. Parachutists, tank and other ground formations were also part of the Air Force: some came into existence almost incidentally, others were raised for a specific purpose.

The General Göring Regiment developed from the Landespolizeigruppe General Göring which in the early 1930s was a para-military bodyguard unit. A number of volunteers were drawn from the regiment in November 1935, received parachute training at Stendal in 1936 and eventually constituted the parachute unit of the General Göring Regiment. In 1938 it became the 1st Battalion of the 1st Parachute Regiment (FJR 1), which later became part of the 7th Air Division of the Air Force (Fliegerdivision 7), which in turn was re-numbered the 1st in early spring 1943. Ten airborne divisions were subsequently formed during the war. 1st Parachute Army, which included two Parachute Assault Gun Brigades, was organised by Generaloberst Student in France in March 1944.

The remaining units of the original Hermann Göring Regiment developed into the Hermann Göring Tank Division another formation of the Air Force, which later during the war was expanded into a tank corps (Fallschirm Panzer Korps).

The Luftflotte was the main tactical organisation of the air force divided into Fliegerkorps and Fliegerdivisionen. The Geschwader was usually commanded by a colonel or lieutenant-colonel and, depending on its assignment could be classified in:

Kampfgeschwader	Bombers
Jagdgeschwader	Single-engine fighters
Zerstorergeschwader	Twin-engine fighters
Nachtjagdgeschwader	Night fighters
Schlachtgeschwader	Air-to-ground attack aircraft
Lehrgeschwader	Tactical, training and experimental aircraft

The Geschwader usually consisted of three Gruppen, each with an average of twenty-seven aircraft and the Gruppe was in turn divided into three Staffeln.

Plate 49. Cap Insignia

All ranks of the German Air Force wore peaked caps, forage caps and from 1943, also another head-dress, with cloth peak, modelled after the Army's mountain cap.

The peaked cap was of conventional German type, with chin strap cords in gold for generals and silver for other officers, and leather chin strap for other ranks.

After Hermann Göring's promotion to Reichsmarschall, in 1940, he started wearing a new pigeon-grey uniform with gold embroidered laurel wreath around the cockade and, often, an additional row of laurel leaves all around the cap band. His new rank badges are shown in the next plate. The generals' cap badges, cords and piping were all made of gold, while the other officers' were made of matt silver. The cockade, oak wreath and side wings, all in one piece were embroidered on black cloth backing, matching the colour of the cap band, while the eagle was embroidered on cloth of uniform's colour.

The same badges but made in aluminium were fitted on the other ranks' cap. A summer service cap with white removable cover and white metal eagle was also used, together with the old style soft, officers' peaked cap without cords above the visor and a tropical cap, all made of brown khaki cloth including the visor, with woven cap badges.

Smaller badges without oak leaves wreath were worn on the other two head-dresses, in gold, silver and grey for generals, officers and other ranks respectively. The latter also wore a composite badge, with the eagle and cockade machine-embroidered on a one-piece of grey-blue cloth. Alternatively, some badges were embroidered on khaki for use on the tropical uniform.

On steel helmets the national colours were placed on the right side and the eagle on the left.

Breast Insignia

The Luftwaffe emblem, the eagle in flight holding a swastika, was worn above the right breast pocket, with its base stitched above the pocket's flap. Several variations of this badge are in existence, embroidered on grey-blue, white, khaki, or in white metal with brooch pin for the white summer uniform.

The rule of gold badges for generals, silver badges for officers and grey woven badges for other ranks, was applied as usual.

Plate 50. Field-Marshals' and Generals' Rank Insignia

On 19 July 1940 Field-Marshal Göring was appointed to the new rank of Reichsmarschall of Great Germany thus becoming entitled to wear a special pigeon-grey uniform with new badges. This uniform consisted basically of peaked cap, tunic with folded collar and buttons covered under a flap, breeches and riding boots. Interlaced gold cords with gold badge were worn on the shoulders and special patches, with gold embroidery on a silver base, appeared on his collar. The gold eagle embroidered on the right patch was replaced in March 1944 by crossed batons, already present on the other collar patch.

The rank of Generalfeldmarschall, or Field-Marshal, was instituted in February 1938 while that of Colonel-General dates back to 1936. The former had gold cords and silver crossed batons on the shoulders while the latter had two gold and one silver cords interlaced on the shoulder and three silver pips. The collar patches of both were similar, depicting the eagle above a wreath in gold, with additional silver crossed batons for the Field-Marshal.

Bar exceptions, the backing to all marshals' and generals' shoulder cords was white and the backing to the Field-Marshals' and other generals' collar patches was also white. The pips were 18 mm. in size, in silver since 1935. The Major-General of the Medical Corps wore the arm-of-service badge instead of the conventional pip, with white backing and since 1944 with dark blue backing under the rank badges. Other colours were granted in 1944 to identify the generals of some other branches of service.

Administrative officials with the rank of general had white and dark green backing under their shoulder cords and dark green collar patches with gold embroidery. The white colour identified their rank and the dark green the branch of service. Also other colours were used instead of white during different periods, as specified below:

Red	15.4.1935–23.10.1935
Black	23.10.1935–1.4.1937
Red	1.4.1937–16.2.1940
White	16.2.1940–1.5.1944
Red	1.5.1944 to the end of the war

The arm-of-service colour of the Court Martial Generals and Judicial Generals Officials were Bordeaux red and wine red respectively.

All collar patches were edged by three narrow gold cords, twisted into one and those of the last three ranks had a gold oak leaves wreath, with from three to one wings embroidered in the centre. Following the German tradition the last rank of the class had no pip on the shoulders.

Plate 51. Officers' Rank Insignia

The shoulder straps and the collar patches had the dual purpose of identifying the rank and the branch of service of the wearer; rank was shown by pips on the former and wings on the latter while the background colour of both identified branch of service as follows:

White	Generals (see below for H. Göring units)
Crimson	General Staff
Golden yellow	Flying personnel and Parachutists
Golden brown	Signals
Scarlet	A.A. Artillery and Ordnance
Dark blue	Medical Corps
Black	Air Ministry (until 1939)
	Construction Troops (from 1939)
Dark green	Administrative officials
Light green	Air Traffic Control
Pink	Engineers Corps (Plate 54)

Officers of the Reserve had additional light blue inner piping on the shoulder straps and collar patches; officers who had served during World War 1 and were subsequently re-enlisted wore an additional light grey inner piping on the shoulder straps only. Retired officers were identified by a stripe of silver lace protruding from under their shoulder straps.

On 23.3.36 all personnel of the General Göring Regiment were issued with standard Air Force uniforms but with white arm-of-service colour. The regiment was formed by two rifle battalions, one of which was a parachute-rifle battalion, and by an anti-aircraft battalion. The N.C.O.s and men of the two rifle battalions wore rifle green piping around their white collar patches, while the gunners had red piping instead.

After the redeployment of the regimental parachute battalion the two remaining battalions were brigaded and in June 1942 the Hermann Göring Tank Division came into existence, with its personnel wearing black tank uniforms and tank patches with skull and crossbones, with white piping. The identification of the various divisional branches of service made necessary the adoption of further colours that from 4 January 1943 were applied as piping to the collar patches, as follows:

White	Grenadier Regiment/Guards Regiment
Pink	Tank and Reconnaissance Troops
Red	Artillery and A.A. Artillery Regiments
Golden brown	Signals Battalion
Light blue	Supply Troops/Administrative Troops/Military Police

All had white piping on the shoulder straps.

In April 1943 white collar patches were adopted for all and the coloured piping was moved on to the shoulder straps, with the following additions:

Rifle green	Rifle Regiment
Golden yellow	Flügbereitschaft Reconnaissance
Black	Pioneer Battalion

The following June the military policemen changed their piping from light blue to orange.

From the end of 1942 the Air Force started to organise Field Divisions, twenty-two of which eventually came into operation, until they were disbanded or transferred to the Army by the end of the next year. The officers wore rifle green collar patches with metal twisted cords and shoulder straps piping in arm-of-service colours while other ranks had a narrow piping also around their rifle green collar patches. The arm-of-service colours were the same as those described above.

The Corps of Administrative Officials included many branches, depending on specialisation, which was identified by the colour of the inner piping of their shoulder straps. During World War 2 all except Court Martial and Judicial Officials had dark green collar patches, all with 3-pointed pips instead of wings; the Court Martial Officials wore Bordeaux red patches and Judicial Officials wine-red patches and inner piping on the shoulder straps. The usual square metal pips were worn on the shoulder straps.

The officers' collar patches were 40–48 mm. wide, 60 mm. in height with a full oak leaves wreath in silver embroidery for senior officers and six leaves and two acorns for junior officers; all had silver cords piping. Rank was identified by small silver wings, one for each successive rank. The shoulder straps consisted of silver double cords, plain for junior officers and interlaced for senior officers. Yellow metal pips, and sometimes numbers and badges were worn on these shoulder straps.

Plate 52. N.C.O.s' Rank Insignia

The titles of these ranks have been transcribed in the original German version due to difficulty and confusion that could be caused by translating these rank titles into English.

The N.C.O.s wore rank badges on the collar and the senior N.C.O.s also on the shoulder straps. On the collar, rank was shown by wings attached to patches of the same colours as those of the officers. The collar patches illustrated were used on the greatcoat as they have the stripe of lace attached on the patch itself, while on the jacket the silver lace was stitched all around the collar instead. White metal pips were worn on the shoulder straps.

Following tradition the personnel of the Artillery used the title of Wachtmeister instead of Feldwebel in their terminology of rank. An additional rank, that of Hauptfeldwebel was used after March 1938: its badges were the same as those of the Oberfeldwebel, plus a stripe of silver lace on the lower sleeves, above the cuffs.

The junior ranks wore additional chevrons on the upper left sleeve instead of the silver stripe of the senior N.C.O.s: the ranks of Hauptgefreiter, Obergefreiter and Gefreiter were used until May 1944, when the title of Stabsgefreiter replaced that of Hauptgefreiter. The latter was never used in the Anti-Aircraft Artillery and in the General Göring Regiment. The title Flieger means flyer, a private of the Anti-Aircraft Artillery was called Gunner and a parachutist Jäger, i.e. Rifleman.

Plate 53. Rank Badges for Flying Field Uniforms
Special rank badges were worn on the upper sleeves of the flying uniforms and overalls: the background of these badges matched the colour of the material of the uniform on which they were worn and therefore grey-blue, sandy brown and others were used by officers and N.C.O.s.

The Field-Marshal and Colonel-General had oval badges with a yellow embroidered eagle on an oak wreath, the former with additional white crossed batons at the base of the wreath. The rank badge of all the others was shown by a combination of wings and bars, in yellow for generals and white for officers and N.C.O.s. The Stabsfeldwebel wore a pip under four wings. Corporals wore their usual chevrons on the upper sleeves.

The personnel of the Corps of Administrative Officials, who were not combat flyers, wore 3-pointed pips instead of the wings and their patches were of a different shape.

Plate 54. Engineering Corps' Rank Insignia
The engineer officers of this corps wore special rank badges on the collar patches and their arm-of-service colour was pink; these badges were introduced on 20 April 1935 but in May 1940 the propellers on the collar patches were replaced by the usual wings, as worn by the flying officers.

A 4-, 3- and 2-bladed propeller identified the actual rank on the collar patches, while large or small wreaths and the metal of embroidery, gold or silver, identified the class of rank as usual. The engineer officers wore normal shoulder straps with pips but of course on pink underlay.

Propellers instead of wings, combined with bars, were worn on flying uniforms: generals had yellow insignia, while officers wore two or one bar with propellers according to rank.

Plate 55. Musicians' Rank Insignia

The Bandmasters had special rank titles and were identified by distinctive rank badges; the former have been translated into English according to their meaning and the title 'Inspizient' has been translated as Super-intendent.

Rank titles and badges were changed a few times from 1935 onwards. Initially the following ranks existed:

Music-Superintendent (Musikinspizient)
Staff Music-Master (Stabsmusikmeister)
Senior Music-Master (Obermusikmeister)
Music-Master (Musikmeister)

and Bandsmen. The rank of Music-Leader (Musikleiter) was instituted then, because there was a shortage of music-masters.

The Music-Superintendent belonged to the category of officials and therefore he had double underlay under the shoulder cords. The inner underlay was red from April to October 1935; it was then changed to black and back to red again in April 1937. The other ranks wore under-lay in arm-of-service colour. The Music-Superintendent supervised all matters connected with music at the Air Ministry. The music-masters were classed as 'Portepee Uffz' before 1938.

A general reorganisation took place in 1938 and the top rank was divided into two grades:

Senior Music-Superintendent (Obermusikinspizient)
Music-Superintendent (Musikinspizient)

both classed in between the officers and the N.C.O.s. They were followed by the same ranks as before, but with different rank insignia.

The alternate silver and red cords were adopted at this time in twisted form for the superintendents and straight for the music-masters. The former wore them with black underlay and black collar patches until 30 June 1939, when ordinary arm-of-service colours were adopted instead.

The lyre on the Music-Leader's shoulder straps was added in 1936 and the year after it replaced the usual four wings on the collar patches. Bandsmen could attain any rank up to Stabsfeldwebel or Stabswachtmeister while fifers and drummers could reach ranks up to Haupt-gefreiter only.

Bandsmen on duty wore the uniform of their unit with 'swallownest' type epaulettes in arm-of-service colour and additional lace and fringes according to rank and unit.

Plate 56. Cuff Titles

The personnel of some special formations wore an embroidered armlet above the cuff of the right sleeve. The officers' version was embroidered in silver and the other ranks' in grey thread; the officers and N.C.O.s of the Rgt/Div. Gen. Göring, H. Göring and Fallschirm-Jäger Rgts 1–2 had additional edging stripes of silver and grey thread respectively.

The general idea was to name an air formation after a World War 1 ace, a party hero or otherwise to identify a special unit. As all are self explanatory no captions have been added and the illustrations have been arranged in order to take advantage of the space available as much as possible.

The lettering was usually on dark blue, except for the titles of the Parachute Division (Fallschirm-Division) and Parachute Rifle Regiments (Fallschirm-Jäger Rgt 1–2) the backgrounds of which were dark and light green respectively.

One cuff title commemorated the German Condor Legion that partici-pated in the Spanish Civil War and another was worn by those who served in North Africa. Two versions of the Hermann Göring title existed, one in Gothic and the other, a later type in Latin capitals. Göring's regiment was granted the General Göring cuff title which was changed later to the Hermann Göring pattern for brigade, divisional and later, army corps personnel.

Other cuff titles were worn as well, one with the inscription 'Kriegs-berichter der Luftwaffe' was worn by officers only, another one with the inscription 'Tannenberg' was used by all ranks of the Aufkl. Gruppe 10. The cuff title 'Führer-hauptquartier' or 'Führerhauptquartier' was made initially with gold and later with silver lettering; it was worn on the left sleeve.

Plate 57. Commemorative Cuff Titles

The two armlets illustrated were worn by ex-members of famous World War 1 formations commanded by Oswald Boelcke and Freiherr Manfred von Richthofen.

Boelcke after shooting down forty enemy aircraft died in an air collision in October 1916 while von Richthofen at that time was a member of the former's squadron 'Jasta II', before assuming his own command in the following February. Later he took command of a group of squadrons and on 21 April 1918 was shot down and fell behind the British lines. He had been credited with eighty victories, of which seventy-nine were over British planes.

Qualification Badges and Awards

The first badge in the centre of this plate was adopted officially in January 1935, for Pilots and Observers of the newly formed Luftwaffe. It used to be worn, as were most of these badges on the left breast pocket or just below by holders of the Iron Cross 1st Class. Some new badges were introduced in March 1936 for Pilots, Observers, Pilot/Observers and for Wireless Operator/Air Gunners.

However, some of these were used before their official sanction, by qualified members of the German Air-sport Association.

The Air Gunner/Flight Engineer's badge was instituted in June 1942, while unqualified Air Gunners who had participated in at least ten operations in that role were granted a similar badge, but made of reversed metals, in April 1944.

Parachutists were issued with badges in November 1936 and Glider Pilots in December 1940. The former wore theirs on the left pocket. On 26 March 1936 a special badge was granted to aviators who had been honourably discharged from flying duties: appropriately it depicts an eagle standing on a rock, the whole surrounded by the usual wreath.

All the other badges illustrated in this plate were given as an award to non-flying personnel of the Luftwaffe and were worn on the left breast pocket, or below the Iron Cross 1st Class. All were adopted during the course of the war. The Ground-Combat and Tank Battle badges were adopted in 1942 and 1944 respectively for personnel of the ground divisions formed and manned by the Air Force. Higher grade awards of both badges were instituted in November 1944, with numbers (25, 50, 75, 100) at the bottom of the wreath to identify the number of combat engagements in which an individual had taken part. A black tank badge with matt silver eagle was worn by crews of armoured vehicles other than tanks (reconnaissance units) and personnel of 'Panzergrenadier' formations.

The Anti-Aircraft badge was an award primarily given for shooting down enemy aircraft or cooperating in this purpose. It was instituted in January 1941 while the last badge illustrated, which was also the last to be instituted on 27 November 1944, the Sea Battle badge, was created for the benefit of the Air Force's sea branch.

Plate 58. Qualification Clasps

These clasps were instituted on 30 January 1941 for wearing on the left breast, above service ribbons; they were in fact awards given for a number of specific operational flights. The issue of clasps was modified during the course of the war and therefore only the final, definitive set of clasps have been illustrated.

The badge consisted of a central device surrounded by a wreath, with a spray of oak leaves on either side. Cloth versions could be worn as well as metal ones. Bronze, silver and gold identified the class of the clasp, parts of which were made of bronze or were black according to qualification.

In June 1942 a gold pendant was added to the gold clasp as a reward for further operational flights, up to 500 in the case of Fighter and Transport formations. Later, in 1944 the pendant was replaced by a tablet with the appropriate number of operations inscribed in its centre. The lowest number was 200, and increased by 100 at a time: only one tablet could be worn below the clasp.

The Ground Combat clasp was instituted on 3 November 1944 for ground personnel who had taken part in close combat: the central device was made of silver while the rest of the badge was in bronze, silver or gold for 15, 30 or 50 days respectively of close engagement with the enemy. Those wounded in action received the badge for shorter periods.

Speciality and Trade Badges and Awards

These badges were worn by N.C.O.s and men on the left forearm and as a rule they identified a specialisation or trade; the Anti-Aircraft personnel badge, however, was worn as a meritorious award only by those eligible for it.

The device was embroidered in matt silver or grey thread on a grey-blue backing and some N.C.O.s' badges had an additional edging of silver twisted cords.

Plate 59. Speciality and Trade Badges

Other badges have been illustrated in this plate as well as the above mentioned: crew men specialised in Sound Location or Range Finding were entitled to gold edging around their badges after one year of meritorious service and standard bearers wore a special badge on the right upper arm. The crossed flags were embroidered in colour according to the branch of service of the wearer.

N.C.O.s' School graduates wore the 'US' initials on the right forearm. The A.A. Artillery badge was worn on the left sleeve in the period between October 1936 and July 1937 only; the badge illustrated in the previous plate was used later.

Czechoslovakia

Plate 60. Cap Badges

Czechoslovakia became an independent republic after World War I and subsequently managed to build up a considerably strong air force which technically was a corps of the Army.

All ranks' uniforms were khaki, with army type badges but with distinguishing light blue arm-of-service colours shown by means of piping and stripes.

The officers wore gold metal cap badges, the N.C.O.s silver ones and the rank and file wore bronze badges. The latter's badge depicted the Czech Lion on a shield, while the higher ranks had the shield superimposed on a square diamond-shaped base (sides 31 mm.), with or without crossed swords for combatant and non-combatant personnel respectively.

All officers' peaked caps had gold twisted chin strap cords and the generals wore an additional gold embroidery on the visor while the others had a plain visor covered by khaki material. The rank and file wore a forage cap with the badge on the top, left side.

Rank Badges

The badges of rank were placed on the shoulder straps of all officers and other ranks, with the exception of generals who had special embroidered straps and who wore their rank stars on the sleeves, above the cuffs. The generals' embroidered ornaments on the peaked cap's visor, on the collar patches and shoulder straps repeated a lime leaves motif, the emblem of Czechoslovakia.

There were four senior and four junior officers: the former were identified by a gold embroidered stripe all around the loose sides of their shoulder straps and wore from one to four gold embroidered 5-pointed stars. The junior officers had plain straps with piping and from one to four 3-pointed stars.

The N.C.O.s were divided into senior and junior ranks; the former included the Warrant Officer, the Staff Sergeant and Sergeant whose rank was identified by rectangular silver badges until 1938 and later by 3-pointed silver stars.

The rank of Staff Warrant Officer was instituted in March 1939. Buttons with or without crossed swords were used by the personnel of combatant and non-combatant units respectively and gold, silver and bronze buttons were worn according to the type of metal of the cap badge.

Plate 61. Rank Badges

The N.C.O.s' rank badges were placed on the shoulder straps, on an additional light blue stripe which in the case of the senior ranks was sewn along the centre and for the junior ranks across the outer ends of the straps. Career junior N.C.O.s, on long term enlistment, wore both stripes.

In 1938 the rectangular badges of the higher ranks were replaced by silver 3-pointed stars, and later the rank of Staff Warrant Officer was also introduced, identified by a single silver 5-pointed star.

The junior N.C.O.s wore from one to four plain round silver studs on the outer ends of their shoulder straps.

The cadets of the Reserve Officers' School had other ranks' shoulder straps with light blue piping, junior N.C.O.s' studs on the light blue stripe and additional silver lace stripe at the bottom or on both sides of the latter according to graduation. The officer candidates of the Military Academy wore on the outer end of the shoulder straps a gold stripe, 10 mm. wide, for each year of attendance, while flight cadets had blue stripes instead. The same light blue stripe but arranged in a loop was worn at the Flight Specialists' School.

There is a great amount of confusion about the rank insignia of the senior N.C.O.s, due to contradictory information relating to this complex period of Czech history. Germany annexed the Sudetenland in autumn 1938, and the rest of Czechoslovakia in the following March. Armed forces personnel fled to neighbouring countries and eventually to France and to Britain. Others found their way to the Middle East. Rank insignia were often modified for wearing on new uniforms and the 3-pointed star, which could not be found abroad, was replaced by a 5-pointed star. Czech cap badges were eventually made in Britain.

Qualification badges

Qualified Pilots and Observers wore special metal badges on the right breast of the jacket. Crossed cannons appear on the badges of balloon personnel because balloons were deployed as a means of artillery observation.

The R.A.F. organised four Czech squadrons, the personnel of which wore national titles in the usual manner: embroidered in light blue on grey-blue uniform's colour for officers and light blue on dark blue for airmen.

Finland

Plate 62. Cap Badges

Finland declared its independence in December 1917 and its newly raised armed forces became engaged against the Russians in the ensuing campaign for independence. The Air Corps which was formed in this period later expanded and became eventually an autonomous service.

During World War 2 field grey uniforms of army pattern were widely used although officers and regular senior N.C.O.s wore also a blue service dress which had been adopted before the war. This dress consisted of a peaked cap with gold chin strap cords and embroidered cap badge, single breasted jacket with open collar and four patch pockets with flaps, breeches with riding boots or long trousers and shoes.

The regular officers' cap badge depicted a gold Finnish Lion on a round, protruding red enamel background, on a gold base. On the peaked cap this badge was centred between two sprays of laurel leaves, below an eagle in flight; on other head-dresses the round badge was worn on its own or below a round cockade in the national colours, white, blue and white.

The cockade of N.C.O.s, also used by officers, was made of coloured enamels while that of the other ranks was made of tin metal and painted in the national colours. Another cap badge similar to that of the officers but for lower ranks depicted the Lion and was all made of metal like a button, for wearing on a head-dress which required two badges.

Officers' Rank Badges

The officers of the Air Force wore two different types of rank insignia according to uniform: rank badges of army pattern, on branch of service collar patches were used on the tunic of the field grey uniform while gold stripes were worn on the front of the forearms, above the cuffs of the blue jacket. Stripes were also used on the greatcoat and, sewn on a removable patch, they were attached by means of two buttons on the forearms of the leather coat. These stripes have already been dealt with in another volume of this series on Army badges. The generals wore narrow stripes above a large one, the senior officers wore narrow stripes below a medium one and the junior officers had only narrow ones; the captain wore two narrow stripes with a still narrower one in between.

The collar patches of the field grey uniform were blue with black embroidered frames differing according to class of rank, and with black fir twigs at the front. The frame of the generals comprised one large and one narrow stripe, the senior officers had two narrow stripes and the junior officers one narrow stripe only.

The generals' individual rank was identified by small gold Finnish Lions and that of the officers by gold roses, larger for senior ranks and smaller, 13 mm. in diameter, for the others. The officers of the services had branch of specialisation badges on the collar instead of the fir twigs.

Qualification Badge

Pilots wore a special badge on the left breast pocket. It depicted a swastika surrounded by six rotating wings, the whole ensigned by a stylised crown. It is noteworthy that the swastika was an old, traditional Finnish-Estonian emblem, unrelated to the then contemporary German swastika.

Plate 63. N.C.O.s' Rank Badges

The N.C.O.s had collar patches in arm-of-service colours but without the fir twigs: rank chevrons were sewn in the centre, a large chevron for the Flight Sergeant and from one to four narrower ones for the other ranks. On field and fatigue tunics without collar patches, chevrons or plain stripes were worn on the shoulder straps.

A winged propeller was the arm-of-service badge of the Air Force and was worn on the shoulder straps, in the case of officers above a gold metal lion.

Poland

Historical Background

Poland regained its national independence in 1918 after World War 1 and due to the precarious circumstances of that time it started immediately to organise armed forces to defend its new status.

However, Polish aviation history dates back to the years before 1918: Adolf Warchalowski, for instance, held the Austrian Pilot Brevet No. 1; two Poles were among the first six Russian officers to train as pilots in France in 1910, and Wlodzimierz Mazurkiewicz, also a Pole, was in fact Bulgaria's first pilot; he flew during the Balkan War 1912–13 and later became a flying instructor in the Chinese Army.

Before World War 1 Poland was partitioned between Russia, Austria and Germany but enthusiasm for flying knew no boundaries and later, during the war, it became the common denominator among Poles fighting under different flags.

The Russian Revolution gave an opportunity to the Poles in the East to organise their own units which often became entangled in local events and also found their way home barred by the Austrian and German armies. The 1st and later the 2nd Polish Combat Aviation Unit were raised at that time in Russia, but both were eventually captured and disarmed by the Germans. In the meantime Polish aviators were trained in France where eventually they formed seven squadrons comprising about 100 aircraft, which in 1919 were sent to Poland.

By the end of October 1918 the Poles started to take over control of their own country from the Central Powers which were collapsing. Military installations and airfields were occupied by local Polish soldiers and volunteers which together with others who arrived from Russia, France and other countries, eventually constituted the Polish armed forces that in the next few years secured Poland's independence.

One of the first aviation units to be raised at that time which became internationally famous, was the 3rd Aviation Squadron, formed at Rakowice Aerodrome, near Krakow, in November 1918. It was redesignated the 7th Aviation Squadron on 21 December and the 7th Kościuszko Air Squadron in the following year, after some American volunteers had joined the unit.

Initially the squadron was commanded by Captain C. Perini and participated in the defence of Lwów and subsequent liberation of the Malopolska.

A group of American aviators, some of whom had been members of

Hoover's Relief Mission at Lwów, while watching the military parade of 14 July 1919 in Paris conceived the idea of offering their services to Poland as Kościuszko had done for the cause of American Independence. In October 1919 the first seven American pilots joined the Squadron which was engaged in war operations from the following April to the end of that war. Later the squadron was transferred to Warsaw, where it was renumbered the 111th and became part of the 1st Regiment.

Initially Polish airmen wore a variety of uniforms, mainly Austrian, Russian or French, but all had the Polish Eagle as their head-dress badge, some examples of which have been illustrated. Those who came from Russia had dark blue uniforms and wore a winged propeller badge on the left upper sleeve while those from France had horizon blue uniforms of French pattern but with the square-shaped czapka instead of the kepi. On this head-dress they wore the Polish Eagle and below, on the cap band, they wore the rank stripes set on a padded oval 3 × 4 cm. in size. The officers wore an eagle, embroidered on a red circular background on the shoulder straps; this badge was also used as a beret badge. They had French aviation collar patches with the 5-pointed star followed by a wing, in the shape of a falling star.

The Polish aviators' uniforms of units formed in the former Russian and Austro-Hungarian territories developed separately from those of units in the former German territory (Greater Poland). The former units adopted field grey army uniforms but as their arm-of-service colour was dark yellow and that of the military police was light yellow, dark blue uniforms were adopted in January 1919 for the personnel of the Military Aviation. However, by then the other ranks had already been issued with field grey uniforms and the officers continued wearing the uniforms they possessed. Many changes and modifications took place in a relatively short time: the dark blue round peaked cap initially had piping around the top of the crown and along the centre of the cap band; then the second piping was moved to the top of the cap band and later the leather visor was covered dark blue cloth, edged with dark brown leather. The rank badges were also changed and ultimately they were adopted in the form of stars on trefoil-shaped shoulder cords.

Field grey uniforms were worn in the former German territory, with the Polish czapka instead of the round peaked cap. The eagle, but with shield, was worn at the front and a trefoil-shaped silver ornament on the left side of it. On the round peaked cap of the uniforms previously described the usual eagle above the shield was worn and a white and red metal cockade was attached to the cap band.

Other significant insignia introduced during this period are the arm badges for flying personnel: i.e. an eagle in flight embroidered in silver or made of white metal, on dark yellow background, was worn by aircraft

178

personnel and a winged anchor by balloon personnel of the former Russian and Austrian territories. In the ex-German territory some dark blue velvet collar patches with yellow piping were used instead. A silver wing and an anchor with wing were shown on these patches by aircraft and balloon personnel respectively. A silver embroidered winged propeller on yellow background was also worn on the left upper sleeve.

New regulations appeared on 27 December 1919 and during the following year all army uniforms were standardised to a new khaki pattern; the Military Aviation was part of the Army and therefore conformed to the rule.

Square peaked caps with brown leather visor and chin strap were introduced; the visor was edged by a white metal rim and the new cap badge was slightly larger than the previous pattern. Dark yellow collar patches with 'zigzag' ornament, differing from the later pattern, were worn on the stand-and-fall collar of the tunic and silver or white metal badges were worn on the left arm.

Rank insignia were initially worn on the cuffs and on the shoulder straps but later the former were abolished. These regulations were strictly applied in order to standardise the Polish uniforms once and for all: by 1 February 1920 all the officers had to wear the new rank insignia and the new caps and by July all had to wear the complete new uniform.

Additions and modifications were prescribed in due course; a dark yellow cap band was adopted in 1930 and the tunic's buttons, for instance, originally five were increased to six and then to seven. Officers and warrant officers and N.C.O.s wore blue trousers with yellow stripes for evening occasions. The former had two large stripes with piping in between while the N.C.O.s had only one stripe on the trousers' sides. A ceremonial dagger replaced the sword in 1924.

Although the Military Aviation remained part of the army, new steel grey uniforms were issued to its personnel in May 1936. The major change was that the new uniform's jacket had an open collar, showing grey shirt and black tie. There was one pattern for officers, warrant officers and sergeants and another one for the other ranks.

Plate 64. Cap Badges (1936)

The steel grey uniforms were adopted on 30 May 1936. The peaked cap was round in shape, with black cap band and black leather visor and chin strap.

The officers' class of rank was shown on the visor by a silver zigzag ornament for generals, double silver stripes for senior officers and one stripe only for the junior officers. Individual rank was identified by silver embroidered stars at the front of the cap band below the cap badge, which was embroidered in silver wire.

The other ranks had an oxidised white metal cap badge and wore small replicas of their shoulder straps' rank insignia on the cap band: these insignia were in this case embroidered in silver on black felt. The Warrant Officer wore one silver star, like the 2nd Lieutenant but had no stripe on the visor. Later, by 1939 the N.C.O.s' badges were changed to the army's pattern, slightly smaller, and embroidered on red felt, as already illustrated in another volume of this series.

Rank badges were also worn on the left side of the black beret, but it had no cap badge. The officers' badges were similar to those they wore on the shoulder straps; the Warrant Officer had a silver star above a 30 mm. long red stripe and the others wore the same insignia, chevrons or stripes, as on the peaked cap's band.

Plate 65. Officers' Rank Badges

The officers' steel grey jacket was single-breasted with four patch pockets with flaps and oxidised white metal buttons. A grey shirt was usually worn but white shirt was worn on evening dress; the neck tie was always black. Steel grey trousers or breeches were used in different circumstances, the latter with black riding boots.

The generals had a silver zigzag on black background on the cuffs of the jacket and black 15 mm. double stripes with black inner piping on the trousers while the other officers wore a 15 mm. stripe on the cuffs and trousers. The arm-of-service colour of Doctors and officers of the Commissariat was cherry red and royal blue respectively and was worn in the form of piping on the cuffs and trousers.

The basic rank badge of all officers was the silver embroidered 5-pointed star and stars were worn on the shoulder straps above the generals' zigzag, above the senior officers' double bars or on their own by junior officers. The zigzag and the double bars were embroidered in silver at about 15 mm. from the outer seam; the latter were 15 mm. in width.

Regular and Reserve officer cadets wore different shoulder straps and as they could attain N.C.O.s ranks, chevrons and stripes were worn accordingly, in silver lace by the former, and silver with red edging by the latter. The shoulder straps of the regulars had silver piping while the piping of the reserve cadets consisted of white and red twisted cords. They wore cuff stripes the same as the army cadets; the stripe of the Reserve officer cadets after training was made of silver but had a narrow red strip along its centre.

The Regular officer cadets had black stripes on the trousers; up to the 3rd year's course they wore narrow stripes, 2 mm. wide, exactly the same as those of the N.C.O.s and subsequently the officers' stripes. All had special badges on the collar and the regulars wore badges on the shoulder straps as well; the initials 'SP' mean 'Szkola Podchrazych', i.e. Officers' School.

Plate 66. Warrant Officers' and N.C.O.s' Rank Badges and Miscellanea

The Warrant Officer and regular N.C.O.s wore officers' type uniforms, the former with officers' stripes on the cuffs and trousers, the regular N.C.O.s with a 2 mm. wide black stripe on the trousers only. The others had steel grey uniforms of 1936 army pattern.

The Warrant Officer and senior N.C.O.s (Staff-Sergeant and Sergeant) were identified by a silver lace stripe edged in red on the loose sides of the shoulder straps; the former wore an additional star, while the sergeants had chevrons. The junior N.C.O.s wore from one to three stripes on the shoulder straps. As already mentioned, all wore rank insignia on the head-dress also.

On flying suits different rank badges were worn on the forearms. They consisted of the usual stars combined with zigzag or double bars, or chevrons, according to rank applied in the centre of a cloth roundel with silver edging.

The officers' dress belt was made of black silk and had an oxidised silver buckle, with fittings at the front. The actual belt was 45 mm. in width and the buckle measure 52.5 mm. in diameter.

The pilots of the Reserve who volunteered for additional flights, in excess of the normal compulsory period of flying when on duty wore an armlet on the left upper sleeve of their civilian clothes. The armlet was made of steel grey cloth, 80 mm. in width, with an eagle and the initials 'OR' on the left and the rank insignia on the other side as illustrated. Double bars, stars, chevrons and stripes identified rank as usual; the Warrant Officer had one silver star and a red stripe.

Plate 67. Cap Badges Worn After 1939

On 1 September 1939, the day of the German attack, the Polish Air Force had 397 first line combat aircraft which fought gallantly during the following weeks until the 17th when all hope was lost after the Soviet invasion from the East. Following General Headquarters' instructions, personnel and aircraft commenced evacuation to neighbouring countries, mainly to Rumania.

The vast majority of Polish airmen eventually made their way to France, where General Sikorski had formed the Polish Government in exile. In

December, the first Polish contingents were transferred to Britain in accordance with previous agreements.

On 22 February 1940 the Polish Air Force became an independent service, its personnel in France was re-organised and eventually, by the following May they manned four fighter groups, two reconnaissance groups and one bomber group. The German offensive of May 1940 caught these units still in the process of training and only some fighter formations were able to take part in the subsequent campaign.

During the months of June and July, about 5,500 Polish airmen arrived in Britain from France, adding to the 2,300 who had been admitted earlier.

The Air Ministry had initially decided to recruit Poles in Bomber Command only, but eventually some better terms of collaboration were secured by the Polish Government, then in Britain. Initially an autonomous Polish air organisation was set up within the R.A.F. and all airmen became part of the R.A.F.V.R.; officers were all commissioned to the rank of Pilot Officer, regardless of their previous position.

However, on the strength of a new agreement signed on 5 August 1940 the Polish Air Force became a nationally independent organisation and by the end of that month Nos. 302 and 303 fighter squadrons were operational. Other squadrons were raised during the course of the war as described in the following pages (Plate 73).

Polish aviators wore basically French uniforms during the first phase of their exile: officers had uniforms of Polish pattern made with French 'Louise bleu' cloth while the other ranks wore the available French uniforms. All wore Polish insignia.

Grey-blue R.A.F. uniforms were issued to the Poles in Britain and were worn with the usual Polish cap badges, in silver embroidery for officers and Warrant Officers and oxidised white metal for other ranks. Badges were eventually made in Britain and some variations to the original pattern also appeared; gold and silver embroidered badges were worn by the officers and W.O.s. The peaked cap's visor ornaments were changed to rows of gold embroidered oak leaves for generals and colonels only, following R.A.F. custom.

Polish Eagles of Air Force or Army patterns were used on the forage cap while the other ranks in the R.A.F. usually wore the brass cap badge of the R.A.F.

Shoulder Flashes (After 1939)

The first Polish contingent to train in Britain was issued with R.A.F. uniforms and the Polish Eagle was worn on the left breast pocket. Nationality titles soon appeared in the usual pattern, with light blue lettering on grey-blue background for officers and light blue on dark blue or black for airmen. There were straight and curved titles for the latter, for wearing above the R.A.F. Eagle on the upper sleeves, and a third variation existed with the title and the Eagle on the same background.

In order to encourage the influx of Polish volunteers, Poles residing in other countries, some special arm badges were adopted: they depict the Polish Eagle above a wreath containing the flag of the country of the volunteer's former residence. Four different badges were adopted for volunteers who had been living in France, Belgium, and North and South America.

Plate 68. Officers' Rank Badges (After 1939)

Officers wore standard R.A.F. grey-blue service dress or battledress with additional Polish rank patches on the collar. Gilt buttons with the Polish Eagle were used on the service jacket and British stripes on the forearms, while the stripes were worn on the shoulder straps of the battledress and of the greatcoat, according to R.A.F. regulations.

The rank patches worn on the collar measured about 60 × 25 mm. in size and were made in the shape of a shoulder strap, with gold embroidered small zigzag, double bars and stars, according to rank.

Army rank titles were used by the Polish Air Force contrary to R.A.F. custom but ranks were equivalent, except for that of Air Commodore which did not exist in the Polish Air Force. However, as the ranks on the collar and those on the sleeves showed Polish and British commissions, unrelated to each other, often the two ranks of an officer differed one from the other. As initially all Polish officers were granted the rank of Pilot Officer, many showed a higher rank on the collar patches or, vice versa, many officers rose in rank faster in the R.A.F. than in their own organisation.

The following was the rank comparison between the Polish Air Force and the R.A.F. in October 1941:

P.A.F.	R.A.F.
General	Air Chief Marshal
General of Division	Air Marshal
General of Brigade	Air Vice Marshal
—	Air Commodore
Colonel	Group Captain
Lieutenant-Colonel	Wing Commander
Major	Squadron Leader
Captain	Flight Lieutenant
Lieutenant	Flying Officer
2nd Lieutenant	Pilot Officer

As, however, there was no Polish General/Air Chief Marshal and as on the other hand the need existed to standardise British and Polish ranks, in May 1944 the generals' ranks were all lowered by one; i.e. the General comparing to the Air Marshal, the General of Division to the Air Vice Marshal and the General of Brigade to the Air Commodore.

Chaplains and Bandmasters wore their old badges (Plate 65) on the lapels of the jacket, while Doctors and Dentists wore R.A.F. badges (Plate 2). Regulations prescribed the wearing of the Medical badge without the crown but usually the crown was used as well. Generals and staff officers wore a small Polish Eagle on the cuffs above the stripes.

Plate 69. Warrant Officers' and N.C.O.s' Rank Badges (After 1939)

Also the Warrant Officer and N.C.O.s wore bi-national rank insignia as did the officers. On the collar they all had rank patches which in the case of the Warrant Officer and senior N.C.O.s had additional gold edging at the top and on the sides. The edging, chevrons and stripes were made of gold lace or were embroidered in yellow thread. The Warrant Officers' star was embroidered in gold wire or yellow thread matching the type of edging. A patch with edging and star of gold embroidery has been illustrated.

Aspirant Officers wore special patches with a stripe along the centre, while officer cadets, who graduated, wore N.C.O.s' collar patches with an additional silver edging. Officer cadets in training were identified by white and red twisted cord around their collar patches, as illustrated.

British type of rank badges were worn as well on the forearms by Warrant Officers and on the upper arms by the N.C.O.s. The former used three badges. In 1941 regulations prescribed the wearing of a large button on a black round patch of material superimposed on a larger light blue one, changed in 1944 to an embroidered cap badge but usually the normal R.A.F. insignia was worn instead.

Accordingly, the Polish regulations prescribed the wearing of a small button and later a metal eagle instead of the crown above the Flight Sergeant's chevrons, but the crown was worn as well. Three or two chevrons or the usual 2-bladed propeller were worn by the other ranks.

Plate 70. Qualification Badges

All the Polish qualification badges worn from 1919 to 1945 have been illustrated together for the purpose of clarity and because even very early patterns were worn during World War 2 by those who still possessed them.

All depicted an eagle in flight, about 65 mm. wide from wing tip to wing tip; most eagles held a wreath in the beak and some clutched symbolic lightnings in their claws according to qualification. The metal with which they were made also identified different qualifications. The wreaths of combat badges were usually made of green enamel, although this ruling was not always observed.

They were worn high on the left breast near the lapel under which a small chain was suspended by means of a hook and, although the eagle itself seemed to be suspended by this chain, in reality it was fixed by means of a screw with nut, at the back of the badge.

The first two badges, of Pilot and Observer, were instituted in 1919 and a third badge was adopted in 1928 for aviators with the dual qualification of Pilot-Observer. Five years later the Pilots and Observers were divided into two classes and new badges were issued subsequently.

More badges were instituted during World War 2 by the Polish Air Force in Britain, to match the half-wings which were issued to R.A.F. personnel.

Plates 71/72. Qualification Badges

Four badges were created in 1942 but due to the advent of other aircrew assignments as the war progressed, a new set of qualifications with relative badges was devised in 1944. These badges carried initials on the wreath to identify each individual specialisation.

Artillery Observers qualified as aircraft Pilots were granted a special badge in 1945; this was the last badge issued during the war.

Qualification badges of different design existed as well, for Air Gunner, Balloon Observer and Naval aviators; all were divided into two classes in 1933.

The Naval Aviation manned seaplanes and its personnel wore navy blue uniforms without any distinctive insignia, except for the Pilots' and Observers' wings. The branch was re-formed in October 1944 and an 'L' was then adopted for wearing in the loop of the cuffs' stripes as a special insignia. Technical officers wore red backing showing between the stripes.

Other Badges

A miscellany of badges, usually worn on the breast pocket of the tunic have been illustrated in this plate. Most were worn in Poland before the German invasion, others later in the 1940s.

The basic air formation was the 'eskadra' which, before the war consisted of nine aircraft; two, three or more eskadras formed a 'dywizjon', a division, which grouped eskadras of the same deployment, i.e. fighters, bombers, observation and army support aircraft. Eskadras of different deployment formed the regiments, which were the tactical units defending the territory of Poland.

The 1st, 2nd and 3rd Air Regiments were formed during the summer of 1921, and were based in Warsaw, Kraków and Poznán, respectively. The 4th Air Regiment was raised at Toruń in 1925, the 5th was formed from units of the former 11th Air Regiment at Lida Air Base which was raised in 1925 and disbanded in 1928. The 6th Air Regiment was raised at Lwów in May 1925.

The badges of the Officers' and N.C.O.s' Schools and of the Staff College were worn in Poland and later, during the war, in Britain as well, while the Balloon and Pilots' School badges were used only in Britain.

The badge of the 55th Eskadra has been illustrated as an example of an unofficial badge, the design of which was based on the emblem painted on aircraft. This formation was the former 24th Eskadra of the 2nd Air Regiment, transferred to the 5th, as part of the 2nd Army Support Division, in 1928.

Plate 73. Squadron Badges

Squadron badges were later authorised in Britain for the following formations which were raised from July 1940 onwards and disbanded as No. 300 Źiemia Mazowiecka Bomber Squadron. This unit, named after the Land of Mazovia, was formed in July 1940 at Bramcote. Aircrew who had flown at least one combat mission could wear a crowned figure 300, in gold for officers and silver for N.C.O.s, pinned on the tie knot.

No. 301 Źiemia Pomorska 'Obrôńków Warszawy' Bomber Squadron. It was a unit of the Land of Pomerania, known as the 'Defenders of Warsaw' which was raised at Bramcote in July as was the former; it ended the war as a transport formation.

No. 302 Poznański Fighter Squadron—formed in July 1940 at Leconfield and was named after the city of Poznań. Its personnel wore a light chocolate brown scarf.

No. 303 T. Kosciuszko's Fighter Squadron—was formed in August 1940 at Northolt. Its personnel wore a scarlet scarf.

No. 304 Prince J. Poniatowşki Źiemia Sląska Bomber Squadron—was formed in August 1940 at Bramcote; was part of Coastal Command and later Transport Command.

No. 305 J. Piłsudski's Źiemia Wielkopolska Bomber Squadron—formed in August 1940 at Bramcote, was named after the territory of Greater Poland.

No. 306 Toruńki Fighter Squadron—was formed in August 1940 at

Church Fenton and was named after the city of Toruń. Its personnel wore a green scarf.

No. 307 Lwówski Night Fighter Squadron—formed in September 1940 at Kirton-in-Lindsey, named after the town of Lwów. Its personnel wore a turquoise blue scarf.

No. 308 Krakówski Fighter Squadron—formed in September 1940 at Squires Gate, named after the town of Kraków. Its personnel wore a white scarf.

No. 309 Ziemia Czerwieńska Army Support and Fighter Squadron—formed in October 1940 and its personnel wore a dark blue scarf with white dots.

No. 315 Deblinski Fighter Squadron—formed at Acklington in January 1941. Its personnel wore a blue scarf.

No. 316 Warszawski Fighter Squadron—formed in February 1941 at Pembrey. Its personnel wore a claret red scarf.

No. 317 Wileński Fighter Squadron—formed in February 1941 at Acklington and named after the town of Wilno. Its personnel wore a blue scarf.

No. 318 Gdański Fighter-Reconnaissance Squadron—formed in March 1943 at Detling and operated in the Mediterranean theatre with 2nd Polish Corps as an army support unit. It disbanded in Austria after the end of the war.

No. 663 Air Observation Point Squadron. It was formed at Eboli, Italy, in September 1943 as part of the 2nd Polish Corps. As it was an army unit its personnel wore khaki uniforms and special collar badges which depicted the red and white Polish aircraft insignia on crossed cannons with a wing at one side.

The Polish Fight Team 'Skalski's Circus' was a very small unit formed in the Middle East, as part of the Desert Air Force.

Japan

Plate 73. Cap Badges of Army and Naval Aviation

The Imperial Japanese Army and Navy each had an aviation branch, the personnel of which wore the uniforms of the parent service with very few additional badges, therefore most of the badges illustrated technically belong to one or the other service and have been illustrated only because they were worn by aviators as well.

Both the Army and Naval Aviation were instituted in 1911 and due to the technological achievements of the 1920s Japan built up a strong air force, including air carriers, during the next decade.

Army aviators wore khaki uniforms and peaked caps with red band or the soft cap with cloth visor, both with the 5-pointed star at the front. Metal, cloth or leather versions of the star were usually worn on the flying helmet as well. Naval cap badges of various pattern, according to rank or type of uniform were used by the personnel of the Naval Aviation.

Plate 74. Rank Badges

Army and naval officers had the same rank titles and were identified by the prefix Army, or Navy, before their rank title. The personnel of naval corps had the corps name before the rank title.

During World War 2 the personnel of the Army Aviation wore the M 98 khaki uniforms adopted in 1938, with rank insignia on the collar. Individual rank was identified by stars on collar patches about 40 × 18 mm. in size. Rank class was shown by gold stripes, commencing with the generals who wore all-gold patches and ending with the N.C.O.s who had only a narrow gold stripe along the centre of their red patches. Privates wore red patches with small metal or embroidered stars to identify graduation. One patch on its own could be worn on the left breast or left upper sleeve or field uniform or flying suits.

The naval aviators wore Navy uniforms and rank badges. They had gold stripes on the cuffs of the blue dress uniform and on the shoulder boards which were worn on the white uniform and overcoat only. Collar patches were worn on blue and on khaki service uniforms. On the former black lace stripes were worn on the cuffs as well. Sky blue was the arm-of-service colour of the Naval Aviation.

Collar patches were worn only by the officers and by the Warrant Officers and were different from those of the Army. They were intended to repeat the pattern of gold stripes shown on the shoulder boards: small silver cherry blossoms identified rank, down to the rank of Ensign. The Midshipman had an anchor on both sides of the collar and a gold stripe, without any cherry blossom on the shoulder boards; the Cadet wore an anchor on both and the Warrant Officers wore a stripe instead.

Plate 75. Petty Officers' and Seamens' Rank Badges

The lower ranks of the Navy wore red inverted 'V' chevrons which during World War 2 were changed to special badges, composed of yellow stripes, a cherry blossom and an anchor, and an additional wreath for the petty officers. The cherry blossom was yellow for personnel of the line, coloured for personnel of the Corps, light blue in the case of the Naval Aviation.

The badge was worn on the upper left sleeve and was usually embroidered on dark blue, although some were embroidered on material corresponding to the colour of the uniform.

Other Badges

The other ranks as well as officers could train to become pilots, and the Bomber Fighter Pilot wore speciality badges, similar in shape to the usual naval speciality badges. These badges were embroidered in red thread on dark blue for blue uniforms and dark blue on white for use on white uniforms.

The aviation badge used by the Army Aviation was worn on both sides of the collar, behind the collar patches, but only in peace-time or in the rear areas. Later their use was discontinued and coloured arm-of-service chevrons, sky blue in the case of aviation, were adopted instead, for wearing above the right breast pocket.

A selection of various badges has been illustrated also, including the Pilot's wings, which were worn above the right breast pocket, and others, mainly patches of aviation schools.

Rumania

Plate 76. Rank Badges
An Army Flying Corps was formed in Rumania in 1910 and again after World War 1, in which the Rumanians were defeated by the Central Powers.

The Royal Air Force, as it was designated during World War 2, adopted the grey-blue uniforms in 1931: the officers wore jackets with open collar, while the other ranks wore tunics with stand-and-fall collar. The cap badge depicted an eagle with spread wings above a wreath, the whole ensigned by a crown.

The officers had gold stripes at the front of both forearms: large stripes of varying width identified generals' and senior officers' class of rank and individual rank was shown by narrow stripes, the uppermost of which was folded to form a square loop. The junior officers had narrow stripes only.

The warrant officers of the flying cadre, known as Adjutants, had their rank badges on the shoulder straps, in the form of stylised wings.

Plate 77. Rank Badges
The Warrant Officer of the ground personnel wore inverted 'V' chevrons on the shoulder straps.

The Sergeant wore one gold lace stripe on both shoulder straps while the Corporal and the Private 1st Class had two and one yellow woollen stripes respectively.

At the beginning of the war these badges were worn in the form of 'V' shaped chevrons on both upper sleeves, those of warrant officers were applied on to a backing in arm-of-service colour.

Arm-of-Service Badges—Collar Patches
All ranks of the Air Force wore collar patches in arm-of-service colour. The generals had special patches, with gold embroidered oak leaves on their own colours, which were dark red for generals of the Army and light blue for those of the Air Force, approximately 75 × 35 mm. in size. The others, officers and other ranks, had plain coloured patches with pointed ends.

The following were the basic colours of the various branches of service, although some changes took place during the course of the war:

Fighter units	Deep green
Bomber units	Deep red
Reconnaissance units	Light blue
Physicians	Cherry red
Engineers	Royal blue
Mechanics	Violet
Aerostation/Signals	Brown
Anti-Aircraft	Black
Schools	Orange

A German wall chart of Rumanian insignia, published in 1939, reports that yellow patches were used by the Reconnaissance units, light blue patches with black piping by the Anti-Aircraft and light blue patches with brown piping were used by signallers.

The personnel of the Seaplane Flotilla wore a gold metal anchor on patches as above.

Qualification Badges
Rumanian aviators wore metal qualification badges on the left breast: the badge of the Pilot depicted the crowned Shield of Rumania between wings, while the Pilots of bomber aircraft had a different badge, initially with the cypher of the reigning monarch, and later with the Shield of Rumania on the breast of the eagle. The Observer had a badge similar to that of the Pilot, but with the King's cypher in its centre.

The same crowned cypher on a sword, sided by wings or an embroidered winged propeller was the badge of the members of the civilian Aero Club.

Hungary

Plate 78. Cap Insignia—Peaked Cap/Forage Cap

The personnel of the Hungarian Army Air Force wore khaki uniforms, many details of which resembled the old uniforms of the Austro-Hungarian Empire.

The uniforms of the Air Force officers, warrant officer and sergeants differed from those of their Army counterparts in many details: first of all the Aviators' jacket had an open collar, rank insignia on the shoulder straps instead of on the collar, and the flaps of the formers' jackets were rectangular while those of Army personnel had three points, of Austrian pattern.

The other ranks had army uniforms with khaki forage cap or beret.

The officers, warrant officers and sergeants wore khaki peaked caps or forage caps: the former carried at the front an eagle in flight surmounted by the Hungarian Crown, in gold or silver according to rank, embroidered on black background. The national cockade and rank stripes were worn at the front of the forage cap, as in the Army.

The other ranks wore a khaki beret with a black tally, with a bronze badge at the front, on a triangular black backing.

The forage cap's cockade showed the red, white and green national colours, which were surrounded by a gold, silver or bronze frame, according to rank. The frame was made of wire embroidery or plain metal. The rank stripes were placed underneath and were shaped like an inverted 'V' chevron with the above-mentioned cockade at the apex. Their setting following the same rules as for the stripes on the shoulder straps, except for those of the lowest ranks, who had white stripes on the shoulder straps, and black stripes on the forage cap.

Plate 79. Officers' Rank Badges

The shoulder straps illustrated were 40 mm. in width and various lengths, according to the size of the jacket's shoulders. The edging consisted of two twisted gold cords, and rank stripes on arm-of-service colours were shown inside.

There were three widths of gold lace stripes, the large to identify the generals' rank class; the medium for senior officers, while the narrow stripes identified individual ranks. The generals had a gold embroidered wreath above the stripes; combat personnel had a 'V' chevron above the stripes, while services personnel wore the stripes only.

The generals had red shoulder straps, while those of the other officers, barring exceptions, were black. The officers of the General Staff wore shoulder straps with a red inner stripe, while the Engineer Officers had shoulder straps made of cherry red velvet; the other officers of Aviation Engineering wore cherry red straps made of felt.

Rectangular Insignia, similar to the shoulder straps but without the rounded ends, were used on flying overalls, for wearing on both forearms.

Qualification Badges

In Hungary there was a qualification badge only for Pilots. It was worn above the right breast pocket of the jacket, and was similar to the cap badge, embroidered in gold or silver for officers and warrant officers, and for N.C.O.s respectively.

Plate 80. Warrant Officers' and N.C.O.s' Rank Badges

The other ranks wore their rank insignia on the shoulder straps, or on the forearms of the flying overalls, in the same manner as the officers. The Aspirant and the Warrant Officer wore the same basic badge as illustrated but with gold or silver edging to the shoulder straps respectively.

The Sergeants wore silver stripes, silver edging and white metal buttons, while the rank and file wore a narrow white chevron and stripes without edging to the shoulder straps. Their buttons were made of bronze.

The winged propeller was worn by the latter on the collar of tunics and greatcoats.

Index

Index

This is not a complete index but it is intended only as a cross reference between illustrations and description.